A BRIEF HISTORY OF
GREENLEE COUNTY

ROBERT A. CHILICKY AND GERALD D. HUNT

THE
History
PRESS

Published by The History Press
Charleston, SC
www.historypress.com

Front cover, top: The Spezia & Spezia building on the right is the home of the Greenlee County Historical Society. Courtesy of the Greenlee County Historical Society; *bottom*: County officials pose on the steps of the courthouse in Clifton. Courtesy of the Greenlee County Historical Society.
Back cover, top: Children and teachers of Duncan Grammar School gather for a picture. Courtesy of the Preservation, Restoration In Duncan's Enhancement (P.R.I.D.E.) Society; *bottom*: Benches of the Morenci open pit mine. Courtesy of Nick Cajero.

First published 2024

Manufactured in the United States

ISBN 9781467155021

Library of Congress Control Number: 2023945789

Notice: The information in this book is true and complete to the best of our knowledge. It is offered without guarantee on the part of the authors or The History Press. The authors and The History Press disclaim all liability in connection with the use of this book.

This book is dedicated to the people of Greenlee County, past and present.

This is an enlarged version of the image on this book's cover.

CONTENTS

ACKNOWLEDGEMENTS

Thank you to the many people who have contributed to this book. Offering a wealth of information were the following: Juanita Álvarez, Bette Antonson, Doug Barlow, Joe Brinkley, Randy Celaya, Bill Cochran, Sandra Ford, Mike Fuller, Frank Mayne, Sharon McCoy, Joe Morales, Vicky Morales, Larry Mortensen, Ed and Max Nabor, Jackie Norton, Keith Redford, David Snodgrass, Marsha Sowder, Mark Vinson, Dora and Jacque White. Those who were extremely helpful with loaning us treasured pictures are the following: Larry Barney, Leslie Daniels and the Warren and Emma Barney Family; John Basteen Jr., Deborah Mendelsohn and Dianne Vandell of the P.R.I.D.E. Society; Robert S. Black III; Nick Cajero; Alicia Guerra; Victoria Harriman and Don Lunt of the Greenlee County Historical Society; Robert Moore; Tom Powers and the Morenci Lion's Club. Lynda Scarbrough helped research last-minute newspaper information and acquired a much-needed photo. The Duncan Centennial Committee and Duncan Historical Book Committee provided valuable information. Assistance came from Kate Fitzpatrick and Perri Pyle of the Arizona Historical Society Library & Archives in Tucson, and Wendi Goen of the Arizona State Library, Archives and Public Records, Archives and Records Management Branch in Phoenix.

A special thank-you goes out to Diane Hunt for helping with editing, and to Elizabeth Chilicky, Erin Chilicky-DeLong and Stephanie Chilicky for scanning pictures. This project was truly a family effort.

Gracias a la señora Fernanda Gallardo por ayudarnos con los acentos españoles.

Much of the information comes from newspapers scanned into newspapers.com, unless otherwise noted. Also, we would not have been able to complete this project if it were not for the many people throughout the history of the county who took the time to photograph something or someone they thought was interesting or important.

Many of the pictures come from the personal collections of Robert A. Chilicky and Gerald D. Hunt.

We hope the history of Greenlee County's important contributions comes out in these pages and inspires others to come for a visit or even relocate to our little corner of the world.

INTRODUCTION

The stories of Greenlee County make up a history as diverse as the people who call this place home. From agriculture and mining in the south, to the great forest-covered Mogollon Rim escarpment to the north, this is a wonderful region of Arizona. The towns of Clifton, the county seat, and Morenci serve the needs of the huge mine that employs several thousand people. The mine supplies the world with copper and other metals needed for a variety of products. From the mine lookout, visitors can view one of the largest open-pit mines in the world. Duncan and Franklin, on the banks of the Gila River, make up a rich agricultural and ranching center. Generations of families have lived here working the land and producing grains, vegetables and fruits and raising livestock. The area has been inhabited for hundreds if not thousands of years, and prehistoric living sites are numerous, with evidence of rock walls, metates, pottery shards and various stone tools. Several other communities, including Metcalf and Guthrie, have proven their importance in the development of the county. Farther north, a day trip up the narrow, winding Coronado Trail, completed in 1926,[1] offers spectacular views of mountains ranges and valleys.

The Spanish and early American exploration of this region was spearheaded by several groups. First, in 1540, the Francisco Vázquez de Coronado expedition passed through the area in search of the Seven Cities of Cíbola. In the 1820s, James "Ohio" Pattie and his father came through with a party of men trapping for beaver along the San Francisco and Gila Rivers. Then, in the 1860s, Colonel King Woolsey and his group of U.S.

Left: The Coronado Trail in the early 1940s. *Courtesy of the Greenlee County Historical Society.*

Below: Workers at a Duncan-area farm threshing grain. *Courtesy of the P.R.I.D.E. Society.*

Miners at one of the many underground mine portals in the Metcalf area. *Courtesy of the Greenlee County Historical Society.*

Army scouts explored Eagle Creek. Another group of soldiers, led by Colonel James Carleton, briefly explored and prospected the area. Territorial governor Anson Pacely Killen Safford led an expedition to Eastern Arizona in 1872, exploring the placer deposits along the San Francisco and Gila Rivers. Around this same time, a military group led by a Captain Chase came through searching for marauding Indians. Heavy mineralization was noted, and an expedition of prospectors led by the Metcalfe brothers came from Silver City, New Mexico, to search for possible mining locations. As a result of the Metcalfe expedition, several mining sites were claimed. Reports from these men and others led more explorers and prospectors to seek their fortune along the rivers and in the mountains.

With this activity, the need developed for services that supported mining. Farming and raising livestock were started along the Gila River with its rich soil. Good grazing land was found throughout the county. Some mining was done in the mountains around Duncan, notably the mines near Carlisle, New Mexico, where future president Herbert Hoover worked as a young man. Farming, however, was the primary reason for the town's growth. There were several large and well-known cattle ranches in the county, including the Lazy B (home of Sandra Day O'Conner) near Duncan and the Double Circle of Eagle Creek. In 1932, the entire county had roughly 17,000 head of cattle; the Double Circle alone had 11,000.[2] Sheep and goat ranches were also located in the surrounding hills. After leaving the mining industry, Baylor Shannon started his own cattle ranch in the mountains above Metcalf. Local ranchers supplied the towns with beef and mutton. John Gatti ran a meatpacking business in Clifton and supplied beef to the men building the Morenci Southern Railway in 1900, charging the company a mere nine cents a pound.[3] Huge cattle and sheep drives came through Clifton as herds were taken to the stockyards south of town to be transported on the railroad to market.

The Greenlee County Cattlemen's Association comprised many of the more important ranchers in the state and had great influence on the cattle business. The association was formed in February 1914. Blue River rancher Freddie Fritz became head of the Arizona Cattle Growers Association. The Greenlee group held their meetings in various places around the county, including Mule Creek, Grey's Peak, Cherry Lodge and Apache Grove. The Greenlee County Cowbelles were formed in 1948, joining the state group, which had formed in 1939. Initially, it was composed of women whose families were in the cattle business, but the group felt it would be good public relations to invite women from outside the business.[4]

Originally, the area was part of Yavapai County, with the county seat in faraway Prescott. When the numerous mines were first being claimed and surveyed, they had to be recorded there, necessitating a multiday trip. More counties would be created and borders would evolve in the next few years. In 1879, Apache County was created and was next to claim jurisdiction over the area.[5] The county seat was initially Snowflake, but it was later moved to St. Johns.[6] Then, in 1881, Graham County was formed, and the county seat was in Safford.[7] It was later moved to Solomonville.

The debate around creating a new county was quite often a heated one and sometimes became violent. As early as 1885, it was being discussed that a new county should be formed from the eastern portion of Graham County. At that time, citizens were against the proposal, and meetings were held in Clifton and Morenci. In part, it was argued that the county "is none too large for the proper administration of its affairs, and a division of this county would increase the burden of taxation, and thereby deter capitalists from investing in the county."[8] A correspondent for the *Clifton Clarion* newspaper, J.T. Fitzgerald, was attacked in Prescott over the idea of division by W.C. Bridwell, who was on the territorial council representing Graham County. Bridwell was upset over a story the newspaper had printed.[9]

Into the 1900s, the idea for county division was again discussed, centering on two key issues: distance and money. Some argued that Solomonville was too far away to conduct business and address legal and financial issues. When residents of Safford started advocating that the county seat should be

The Greenlee County Cattlemen's Association held their meeting at the Princess Theater in Clifton in March 1917. *Courtesy of the Greenlee County Historical Society.*

moved back there, even farther away, that only bolstered the argument for the citizens of the east side of the county to break away and form their own county. Moneywise, the copper companies and railroads were responsible for most of the taxes paid in Graham County.[10] Morenci began to gain interest for county division by 1904. Its delegation selected the name *Douglas* for its petition of the county name, in honor of Dr. James Douglas, president of Phelps Dodge. They also proposed the courthouse to be in New Town and the name of that location changed to *Longfellow*. Clifton initially wanted the county name to be *Colquhoun*, after James Colquhoun, president of the Arizona Copper Company, but after the Morenci proposal came to light, Clifton changed its idea to *Lincoln*, for the former U.S. president. Residents of Clifton, Morenci and Duncan held a meeting to settle on a name and soon organized "A League for the Establishment of Lincoln County." They wrote a list of grievances modeled after the Declaration of Independence, and it was published in the local papers.[11] In the end, and after much debate, a last-minute deal settled on *Greenlee*.

Born in Virginia, Mason Greenlee came to Arizona in 1871 by way of Colorado and was one of the earliest miners to come to the district. Indians

The grave marker for Mason Greenlee at Clifton Cemetery. Unfortunately, his name is misspelled. *Original photograph taken by Alicia Guerra.*

were a problem, as roughly one-third of his party was killed. He went back to Colorado but returned in 1879 and formed the Greenlee Gold Mountain Mining District. The claims were centered in and around Dorsey Gulch, about five miles above Clifton along the San Francisco River. The mines were high producers, and Greenlee believed he had found the greatest gold claims on the continent. The last five years of his life were spent in poor health. He initially refused to leave camp, not wanting to leave his beloved surroundings. As he became progressively worse, his friends brought him to Clifton to receive better medical care. Greenlee's health did improve, and he enjoyed visits from friends and well-wishers. Sadly, he suffered a fall and did not recover. He died on April 10, 1903, at the home of longtime friend Ike Stevens.[12] Greenlee was initially buried in the cemetery on Shannon Hill, but his grave, along with others, was moved to the cemetery in Ward Canyon in 1909.[13] He was well-liked and respected by the people of the district, and it was said no finer man could have the honor of having the county named after him.

After the county was created, the vote for where the county seat would be located was equally hotly contested. Residents of Duncan Valley insisted the county seat be located there. They pointed out that Duncan was the first major town on the train line from Lordsburg, New Mexico. J.L.T. Watters sent a letter to the *Copper Era* newspaper. In it, he highlighted the advantages of having the courthouse there. He offered to donate five acres for the site, which was three hundred yards from the train station. He further pointed out that Duncan was already an incorporated town, which both Clifton (at that time) and Morenci were not. He also noted the advantageous location of the town, built in a beautiful valley through which the Gila River flowed.[14] Residents in Clifton formed the "Clifton County Seat Club" to help enlist support for the town and its efforts.[15] Morenci was considered, but their bid was defeated in the primaries, despite strong support from the Detroit Copper Company and Phelps Dodge. The final vote was held in November 1910. Clifton won the honor with 745 votes to Duncan's 482. With animosity still lingering from the primary election, 247 people from Morenci voted for Duncan, while only

County election announcement in the November 11, 1910 *Copper Era*. *Courtesy of newspapers.com.*

87 voted for Clifton. Citizens of Metcalf voted 81 to 6 for Clifton. Another interesting item is that while all 111 votes cast in Duncan were in favor of their town, 70 Clifton residents voted for Duncan. The other towns in the county voted for the town closest to them, but in the end, the larger population of Clifton prevailed.[16] Although the county was formed in 1909, it took time to negotiate payment of existing taxes and to finalize assets. Greenlee County officially began operating on January 1, 1911.[17]

Several lawsuits over the location and sale of land stalled the construction of the new courthouse. In the meantime, county offices were housed in several locations around town, such as the Hampton building on the Eastside, Casino Hall on Chase Creek and the Armory building in South Clifton. Construction for the Greenlee County courthouse and jail finally commenced in early 1912, and county officials moved into the facility on September 1, 1912.[18] Duncan resident Owen O'Dell helped haul material for the building, including one beam weighing sixteen thousand pounds that supports the second floor. It was hauled up the hill to the construction site by four horses.[19] During the 1983 flood, the *Copper Era* was published here using a typewriter and photocopier, since the paper's facilities were under water.[20] After the flood, there was a push to relocate county offices and build a new courthouse at the Three-Way area about ten miles south of town. There was even a proposal to build a shopping center and hotel there. The courthouse was not flooded, but due to its age, repairs were estimated at $500,000, so it was argued it was not worth the repairs.[21] The plan fell through, and the building was renovated in 1998.[22]

When Arizona was granted statehood on February 14, 1912, every whistle and horn in Clifton blew for several minutes, and there was much celebration throughout the county and state. The office of the *Copper Era* in

Clifton received the telegram, and Mayor George Fraser began announcing the news via telephone. A parade was held through the town, and a grand celebration took place at the Clifton Armory with refreshments, speeches, music and dancing. There was a forty-eight-gun salute in the riverbed near the Arizona Copper Company works in the middle of town.[23] The date for statehood was originally set for February 12 to honor the birthdate of President Abraham Lincoln, who created the Territory of Arizona during his time in office, but it was delayed two days.[24]

The county was heavily impacted by the Great Depression of the late 1920s and the 1930s. The mines closed, and only skeleton crews remained on the payroll. Businesses were under great stress, and many folded. During this time, the town of Metcalf started closing and its citizens moved out. It never recovered. Many residents of Clifton, Morenci and Duncan also moved away. The towns began to revive in the late 1930s, however, when miners and their families started flooding into the district looking for work as the underground mining started converting to open-pit operations. Local governments and schools began to take advantage of federal programs designed to help fund

Statehood celebration in Clifton. *Courtesy of the Greenlee County Historical Society.*

building projects. For example, in 1936, Stanton Stadium in Clifton was built using Works Progress Administration (WPA) funds.[25]

As the country was coming out of the Depression, the United States Congress set up a commission to direct the Coronado Cuatro Centennial and named the states and cities where a major event would be held. For Arizona, the cities of Prescott and Clifton were selected.[26] From August 31 to September 2, 1940, a grand celebration was held called the Coronado Entrada. It commemorated the four hundredth anniversary of Francisco Vázquez de Coronado's arrival and exploration in this part of the state. Jack Belzner narrated the show through the perspective of Pedro de Casteñada as the Spanish explorers searched for the Seven Cities of Cíbola.[27] A production company had come to town several months before to help coordinate the event, train the actors and rehearse the show. Those who had speaking parts recorded their lines prior to the event, and the voices were played over Stanton Stadium's sound system during the show. A three-hundred-foot-long stage was built on the field. All of the actors were area residents, making the event special.[28] The costumes for the 750 actors were very elaborate and cost $18,000. Homes and businesses all over town were decorated, and many events, such as bicycle races and Soap Box Derbies, were also held in conjunction with Labor Day. A huge parade led by Arizona governor Robert Taylor Jones traveled from the far west end of Chase Creek and down Railroad Avenue, ending by the lumberyard near the stadium.[29] Main cast members included Filmore Stanton playing Coronado; Margaret Brubaker playing his wife, Beatritz; Bill Bass as Captain Cardenas; Joe Cislaghi as Captain Alvarado; Satornino Morales as Captain Alarcón; and Herbert Schade as Don Antonio de Mendoza. The entire show cost $100,000.[30] An item of interest on display during the weekend was a copper bowl found by Tom Dees in a cave at Ash Peak near Duncan. Dees had come across a flat rock with an Indian symbol for a spring and an arrow pointing toward the mountainside. He went in the direction the arrow pointed and discovered a cave. There he found the bowl, along with the front piece of a Spanish bolero hat with silver braids and fasteners.[31] The Coronado Entrada was a huge success. The proceeds paid for all of the activities, and the remaining money was donated to local Boy Scout troops and the American Red Cross.[32]

The White Mountains to the north were initially crisscrossed with horse trails between the many ranches. Eventually, wagon roads were improved into roads for motorized vehicles. When the road between Clifton and Springerville was completed, it not only provided greater ease of travel, but also the spectacular trip was unmatched for vistas and beautiful scenery.

Coronado Entrada actors on the courthouse lawn. *Courtesy of the Greenlee County Historical Society.*

The Coronado Trail was initially designated only between Clifton and Springerville, but prior to the dedication of the road, A.H. Gardner of the Huachuca Water Company in Tombstone wrote Peter Riley of Clifton, who was the president of the Clifton-Springerville Highway Association. Gardner asked permission for the towns of Nogales, Tombstone and Willcox to use the name for the roads passing through those towns. Riley brought the matter before the Clifton Commercial Club, and the motion passed.[33]

The early explorers and settlers were men and women of tenacity and vision. Mining is the main industry of the county, but cattle ranching, farming and associated businesses play a vital role in the economy. The history of the county is full of stories of sacrifice and success, all highlighting the unshakable human spirit needed to create good living environments.

DUNCAN AND THE GILA RIVER VALLEY

Harvest of the County

The Gila River Valley of eastern Arizona has a long history of habitation. Indian tribes lived along the river for centuries, taking advantage of the dependable water source and rich soil for farming. The travels of Spanish explorer Francisco Vázquez de Coronado are well-documented. As part of this expedition, Hernando de Alarcón drew maps of the river, calling it Miraflores.[34] In November 1846, the First U.S. Dragoons, commanded by General Stephen Watts Kearny, followed the Gila River as the unit marched to California during the Mexican-American War. They were guided by Kit Carson. Undoubtedly, these early explorations led to people hearing about the area. Those who were brave enough to settle here reaped the rewards, but not without many daunting and dangerous challenges.

EARLY DEVELOPMENT

In 1874, California businessman William C. Ralston came to the Duncan area with a group of men looking to establish farms. Ralston was already in the Shakespeare, New Mexico area, lured by a tale that diamonds could be found. It was soon discovered to be a ruse, but not before Ralston had lost a large amount of money. The group brought with them eighty-two head of cattle and five mules and horses. Of those, sixty-four of the cattle herd were cows. A company was formed called the Ralston Ditch Company. Billy Wilson, Cornelius Murrain, Peter Morrissey and Joseph Galbraith, known

Lunchtime at the Cosper ranch. *Courtesy of the P.R.I.D.E. Society.*

as the "Irish Boys," dug the Ralston Canal and began the first farms and ranches in the county. They grew corn, potatoes, onions and beans and sold their crops to the area military posts. Their homestead was locally known as Irish Boy's Ranch. Several tragedies struck the group. Morrissey was shot and killed in 1877 by a posse searching for him to serve a warrant, claiming he and his group were hoarding water rights. Murrain was killed by Indians in 1879.[35] Ralston also met a violent death, in 1875, drowning in the San Francisco (California) Bay while swimming.[36] A telegraph line was eventually established between the valley and Clifton, and there was a steady stream of traffic to the mines. Soon, other industrious people came to the Gila River Valley and began establishing farms.

The NPB Ranch, named for N.V. Newcomb, Rueben Purdy and George Batchelder, was near the present-day Greenlee County Fairgrounds and was the site of the ranch headquarters. This location was known as Purdy.[37] A post office at the ranch was established in April 1883, with Batchelder as postmaster.[38] A stop for the stage line that ran through Purdy was established. During the 1882 Indian Campaign, the soldiers of Troop D, Sixth Cavalry under the command of a Captain Gordon made camp here while assisting soldiers of the Fourth Cavalry against Indians in Horseshoe Canyon.[39]

Franklin, one of the main settlements, is about three miles southeast of Duncan. It was founded in 1895. The first settlers from the Safford Valley brought their own lumber to construct their homes and businesses. The roughly 3,500 acres of land were considered raw and untouched, even

Purdy ranch hands, 1883. *Courtesy of New York Public Library.*

though farming had been going on in the area for years. Thomas Nations, Ben Echols, Henry Tippets and others constructed the Model Canal, and it extended eight miles into New Mexico. Initially, twelve families came to the area. The first years were challenging, as the first crops failed because of the alkaline in the soil. Water was soaked up before reaching the crops. Families came together and shared harvests and day-to-day farming chores until eventually the fields were made productive.[40] According to the *Graham Guardian* newspaper, the town's name is in honor of Arizona territorial governor Benjamin Franklin.[41] The post office at Franklin was established on May 17, 1905, with Nephi Packer as postmaster. It continued until March 14, 1958, when it became a rural branch of the Duncan Post Office.[42]

RAILROADS

The Arizona Copper Company purchased the mining interests of the Lesinsky brothers in 1883,[43] and it quickly realized that a connecting railroad was needed to ship the smelted copper to ready markets. Copper had been shipped out by wagon over rough terrain. It was slow and expensive and vulnerable to Indian attacks. Several companies were invested in the area, and in early 1883, a rail line was completed between Lordsburg, New Mexico, and Clifton, Arizona. The Clifton & Southern Pacific Railway was on the Arizona side of the border, and the Clifton & Lordsburg Railway was on the New Mexico side.[44] When a train of the Clifton & Southern Pacific Railway made its first stop at Duncan Station on May 20, 1883, there was much celebration. The crowd cheered, and bells were rung, and there were volleys of artillery fire. Many speeches were made, and even the king of Denmark sent Mr. Nels Matson as his personal representative.[45] By the end of 1883, the railroad was completed to Clifton, connecting the mining district and the Gila Valley to the outside world.

In July 1883, the post office was moved from Purdy to Duncan Station, which was along the railroad on the south side of the river. C.A. Boake took over as postmaster.[46] In August of the same year, the rail lines merged to form the Arizona & New Mexico Railway, entirely controlled by the Arizona Copper Company.[47] Soon, support businesses and schools were built. The communities on both sides of the river were consolidated and named Duncan to honor James Duncan Smith, a director of the Arizona Copper Company.[48] As a result of the railroad, the population along the river grew quickly, and the valley's rich alluvial soil helped encourage the establishment of prosperous farms and ranches.

The Duncan Train Station and Section House of the Arizona & New Mexico Railway were always full of activity, with passengers and freight moving through day and night. As the mines developed at Carlisle, New Mexico, Duncan became an important railhead for the Carlisle Gold

A large crowd gathers at the Duncan train station. *Courtesy of the Greenlee County Historical Society.*

Duncan train station under construction. *Courtesy of Larry Barney, Leslie Daniels and the Warren and Emma Barney family.*

Mining Company. High-wheeled baggage carts were used to load and unload the train's freight. Railroad agents working at the depot lived on the top floor with their families. The Section House offered living spaces for railroad workers and stored maintenance equipment for this section of the line. The railroad contracting firm Ward & Courtney, which helped build this line, stored its equipment here. This firm also owned the WC Ranch near Duncan. In 1906, the Section House was valued at $150.[49]

Indian Conflicts

Problems with Native Americans were widespread. Killings of miners, ranchers and their families were common. In April 1882, Apache warriors led by Geronimo broke away from the San Carlos Reservation. They raided several areas, including Eagle Creek, the Detroit Copper Company smelter complex south of Clifton and several places along the Gila River. All told, forty-two people were killed and five wounded. One of the men killed, F.B. Knox, met his end on the York Ranch along the Gila.[50] He was protecting his family, allowing them to escape while he held off the attack as long as he could. This location is known today as Apache Grove.

A group in Clifton, the Clifton Guards, was created in June 1885. They were commanded by Captain T.S. Ford. Clifton businessman Henry Hill was a lieutenant.[51] They were ordered into service to help pursue Indians near Duncan and Carlisle, New Mexico. On receiving the order, the Guards initially went to the Eagle Creek area to investigate Indian activity there. Captain Ford and thirteen of his men then went by train to Duncan to prepare for the engagement. The remaining Guards soon arrived with all the horses and equipment.[52] They received fresh horses from Duncan-area ranches and then headed out in pursuit. They were joined by a group of men from Duncan, led by W.J. Parks. Eventually, the chase wound up in Doubtful Canyon, about forty miles south of Duncan. A gun battle ensued throughout the canyon and went into the night. During the battle, one of the mounted Duncan men saw two figures fall from one of the horses on the Indian side, and his galloping horse had to jump over them. The battle ended, and the men made camp. The next morning, they were headed back to Duncan when they heard what sounded like a baby crying. As they got closer, they realized it was the cries of an Indian baby under what was presumed to be his mother. Parks secured the papoose and took the baby back to his home in Duncan. Mrs. Parks decided to give him a bath. As she was undressing him, she discovered he was wearing the beautiful dress of a White child. The baby was initially given the name "Doubtful," after the canyon where he was found. The formal naming of the young boy was of interest to the territorial capital. A petition was being circulated, to be presented at the territory legislature, to have the young boy named Pache Van Arman. Hyram M. Van Arman was the acting territorial governor at this time, and he wanted to adopt him.[53] The Bill Adams family assumed care of the baby, and they moved to Solomonville, where Doubtful went to school. The family changed his first name to Sam, and he took the family name of Adams. Sadly, he was never fully accepted by the White population or by the Indians. He died of tuberculosis on the San Carlos Indian Reservation in 1913.[54]

The people of Duncan had had enough. Citizens wrote a letter to Arizona territorial governor C. Meyer Zulick, pleading with him for permission to establish a guard force. The letter, governor's response and conditions of enlistment for the men of the force were printed in the December 10, 1885 *Arizona Daily Star*. With this, the Arizona Rangers, so labeled in the newspaper, was formed.[55] The group was also known as the Duncan Rangers, or the Duncan Militia. It was a mounted force of fifty men paid for by the territorial legislature and commanded by Captain W.J. Parks.

Religion

The role that religion has played in the history of the county is immense. In the 1860s, settlers began arriving in the upper Gila Valley. Cándido Tellez, a Las Vegas, New Mexico man, moved to a location near Box Canyon. Others followed, and a Catholic church was built to meet the spiritual needs of the community, which became known as San Antonio. Visiting priests from Clifton conducted masses and performed marriage rites. The ruins of San Antonio and its cemetery are near the home of R.T. John. Tellez established a freighting company and in the 1870s began hauling supplies between the new mining communities of Clifton in Arizona Territory and Silver City in New Mexico Territory. Supplies from Silver City were hauled to Clifton, and smelted copper was freighted on the return trip. The Richmond Mining Company began operating in the area, and San Antonio's name was changed to Richmond. The Tellez Canal is one of the area's oldest canals, providing irrigation water to farms that grew corn and squash.[56]

Mormons, well known for their agricultural successes, began coming to the region with the encouragement of their leaders in Utah. To escape persecution in the United States, many the polygamist families first settled in northern Chihuahua and Sonora at the behest of the Mexican government. They established seven *colonias* and built irrigation systems, churches, farms and beautiful homes. With the outbreak of the Mexican Revolution in 1912, the colonias were no longer protected by the Mexican government, and the residents' farms and livelihoods were under attack and their lives threatened. Many families chose to escape back to the United States, and some of them came to the area in search of a new place to live. They looked to the Gila Ranch and Cattle Company to help them purchase plots of land to create farms and build homes. Earnest W. Virden, owner of the company, helped them acquire land in the Richmond area. Richmond's name was changed to Virden in 1915 to honor him.[57]

The initial group of Methodist worshipers in Duncan came from Richmond, New Mexico. The original church was a frame building erected in 1913.[58] Their next building burnt down in 1946. Undiscouraged, the congregation made plans to rebuild, and the First Methodist Church was dedicated on November 28, 1948.[59] In 1951, artist Hal Empie donated two paintings of Jesus Christ to the church.[60] Today, it is the United Methodist Church.

The First Baptist Church in Duncan was established in 1932. Church services were held in several locations until this building was completed in

Top: Duncan Methodist Church, 1963. *Robert A. Chilicky personal collection.*

Bottom: First Baptist Church in Duncan, late 1950s. *Robert A. Chilicky personal collection.*

Opposite: Mormon church on the corner of Third Street and East Avenue in Duncan. *Courtesy of Larry Barney, Leslie Daniels and the Warren and Emma Barney family.*

the late 1930s. One of the early locations was in a local converted stable. Reverend Bender was reported to have said, "Our Savior was born in a stable, why can't we worship in one?"[61]

The Mormon congregation funded the construction of its chapel largely by selling Mexican-style suppers, crocheted doilies, baked bread and cinnamon rolls. The first service was on December 23, 1952. Even though the building was not completed, members wanted to enjoy their Christmas service here. This building is now Saint Mary's Catholic Church. Across the street from the church once stood a two-story fort used in the early days for protection against Indians and outlaws.[62]

The Duncan Presbyterian Church has an interesting history. In the early 1920s, a deal was struck between this congregation and the Methodists. The Presbyterians withdrew from Duncan, and the Methodists withdrew from Clifton. The Methodists began to meet in Duncan.[63]

BUSINESS AND ENTERTAINMENT

Duncan was at the crossroads of the mines and smelters of Clifton, Morenci and Metcalf; the mines of Carlisle and East Camp, New Mexico; and the farms of the Safford Valley. It was also the connection to the main railroad

E.W. Taylor Store, 1909. C.P. Dunn has hung a campaign sign in his bid for county supervisor. *Robert A. Chilicky personal collection.*

and businesses at Lordsburg, New Mexico. Stores selling goods and services needed to provide a well-stocked grocery section and supply the latest products for customers, and auxiliary services such as hotels and restaurants were in high demand. The E.W. Taylor Store met these needs. It was on the corner of Railroad Boulevard and Main Street. Railroad Boulevard is Highway 70 today. The store became the Duncan Mercantile under the ownership of Stanley Coon for many years. It then became Boyd's Brothers Grocery. The building burned down in 1992.[64]

The Duncan Milling Company, owned by Interstate Farmers Incorporated, was on East Avenue in Duncan. It operated for many years before closing in the 1960s. Joseph Moffett was the company's long-term manager. This business, along with many like it, serviced the extensive agricultural industry in the valley. In the early days, it was operated by the Romney brothers (Ernest, Eugene and Junius) along with the brother-in-law of Junius, Edward Lunt.[65] In 1922, they reached an agreement with the Phelps Dodge Mercantile Company to be the exclusive supplier of flour to the company's stores in Clifton, Morenci and Metcalf.[66] The mill's product was brand-named Golden Poppy Flour.

Lunt's Dairy is located about one half mile west of the Arizona / New Mexico state line in the Duncan Valley. The Lunt family is prominent in the valley, with many farms owned by members of the family. The group of farms the family owned was nicknamed "Luntville."[67] In 1922, George Lunt hosted free picture shows at his farm for local farmers and their families. Shows included *Sweet Potatoes from the Store House to Market* and *Out of the*

Lunt's Dairy. At the door is George Lunt, with Audrey and LaDonna Lunt, daughters of Ed Lunt, on the bicycle. *Courtesy of the P.R.I.D.E. Society.*

Apache Grove entertainment hall, York Valley. *Courtesy of the Arizona Historical Society Library & Archives, Oliver Ambrose Risdon Photograph Collection, PC 204_F.21_B.*

Fish from the Gila River
sometimes made their
way into the canals,
which made fishing
here a favorite pastime.
*Courtesy of the Greenlee
County Historical Society.*

Shadows. He served free ice cream made in his dairy.[68] The dairy delivered and sold many of its products to stores throughout the county.

Apache Grove Dance Hall was once a venue for national and world-famous singing acts. Artists such as Hank Williams, Slim Whitman, Bob Wills and Patsy Cline entertained here. Wrestling matches were also a crowd favorite, with the likes of Gorgeous George prowling the ring. Golden Glove boxing was also hosted here, with Clifton-area boxers, managed by Al Fenn, regularly defeating visiting teams. Clifton boxers such as Tito Carrillo, Hilberto Quintana, Ernest Castañeda, Wilson Yazzie and Johnny Aguirre were feared throughout the state and region. Arizona boxing legend Zora Folley, also managed by Fenn, fought here. The grounds nearby held other events, such as stock-car racing, destruction derbies and the Greenlee County Ministerial Association meetings in the 1940s.[69]

George Phillips built a skating rink in Duncan in 1909.[70] It was located near the blacksmith shop. In 1921, B.F. Billingsley relocated his store here after his business was lost to a fire a few weeks prior.[71]

VISIONARIES

The Duncan area has had its share of important people who helped shape the valley and county. They were men of vision, and their ideas for customer service were evident in their goods and services. Some showed their worth through assertive action when facing a difficult situation. Judge Wiley Aker was one of these men. In the 1930s, the state highway department installed a traffic light at the intersection of Highway 70 and Main Street. Drivers still rolled through the intersection, paying no attention to the light. A loudspeaker was even installed, and an officer tried to alert drivers as they approached, which caused confusion and accidents. Aker himself was once ticketed when he failed to stop at the light. Driving was difficult for him, as he was missing a part of one arm and leg. After pulling off the road, he told the officer that the light would be coming down, and soon after, it did, but only after Aker paid the fine.[72]

Benjamin F. Billingsley was a prominent businessman in Duncan for many years. His store was always stocked with the latest farming machines and tools and a wide variety of groceries. He was elected to the Greenlee County Board of Supervisors and served the people of the county faithfully throughout the years. Billingsley was instrumental in improvements all over the county and had a great career in public and commercial service for the people of Duncan. His brother Joe operated a general merchandise store in Clifton's Hill's Addition (South Clifton), specializing in fresh fruit and vegetables, eggs and dry goods,[73] until 1912, when he sold his stock to W.F. Hagan & Company.[74] The current Bonnie Heather Inn was one of Benjamin's store buildings, rebuilt after a fire.[75]

James Luther Teague Watters owned and operated the first drugstore in Duncan, from about 1901 to 1916, when he sold the building to George Deibert from the Arizona Copper Company drugstore in Clifton.[76] Watters decided to continue his real estate business. He was a man of many trades. In different times in his life he was a judge, a notary public and a postmaster and sold insurance. The home of Watters became the location of the Duncan

Billingsley store (*center*) and the train depot (*right*). *Courtesy of the P.R.I.D.E. Society.*

Opposite, top: Home of Benjamin F. Billingsley on Main Street. It is listed in the National Register of Historic Places. *Courtesy of the P.R.I.D.E. Society.*

Opposite, middle: J.L.T. Watters standing in front of the post office. *Courtesy of the Greenlee County Historical Society.*

Opposite, bottom: The Freiheit building was a part of Spezia Corner. *Robert A. Chilicky personal collection.*

Above: Hal Empie postcard, 1937. *Robert A. Chilicky personal collection.*

Post Office when he became postmaster on September 13, 1897. He served until 1934. For a time, the post office was near the current location of the Bonnie Heather Inn. It moved to its present location in 1941.[77]

Hart Haller "Hal" Empie was a world-renowned artist. He was born near Safford, Arizona. When he was young, his family moved to Safford, and his parents opened the New York Hotel. At the age of twelve, he worked at the Best Drug Store in Solomonville and later studied at the Capitol College of Pharmacy in Denver, Colorado. After passing exams, he became the state's youngest licensed pharmacist at the age of twenty. He moved to Duncan in 1934 and served as interim manager of the Duncan Drug Store. In 1959, he opened Art Gallery Drug, which he operated until 1986. Later, he moved to Tubac, Arizona, and opened the Hal Empie Studio and Gallery.[78] His paintings and cartoons depicting western life and humor have been used in numerous publications and are sought out by collectors.

The Spezia family of Clifton had a big influence in Duncan business and banking. Around 1915, the firm of Spezia & Spezia constructed buildings on Hill Street near Railroad Avenue. It was known then as Spezia Corner, but today it is called Spezia Square. In 1921, the buildings in this section of town suffered great fire damage. The fire was discovered in the predawn hours. A young couple staying in a room above Billingsley's store made it onto the street just before the second floor collapsed.[79] Charles and Ambrose Spezia were on the board of directors of the Bank of Duncan, which was located next to the Simpson Hotel. Charles also served as the bank's vice-president.

HOTELS AND SALOONS

Weary travelers passing through the valley, or those visiting the area, could find a comfortable room or enjoy nightlife at one of the several hotels and saloons. The Duncan Hotel, operated by Mrs. W.S. Munday, was such a place. The hotel was billed as "everything neat and clean and a good meal served at reasonable rates."[80] In 1902, the manager of the Ash Peak group of mines had his office at the hotel.[81] The venue served a lavish Thanksgiving dinner in 1907 for fifty cents.[82]

The Simpson Hotel, built in 1914, was initially named the Hobbs Hotel, for owner Gus Hobbs. It had twenty rooms, each with a fireplace and a private bath.[83] In 1915, W.T. Witt, chairman of the county's board of supervisors, purchased it for $11,000, and the hotel took his name.[84] In

An early version of the Duncan Hotel. *Courtesy of the P.R.I.D.E. Society.*

The Simpson Hotel continues today as an exceptional bed-and-breakfast and is routinely featured in state tourism publications. *Courtesy of the P.R.I.D.E. Society.*

This view looks north toward the bridge over the Gila River. The Duncan Saloon and Gardner Hotel are on the left. *Courtesy of the Arizona Historical Society Library & Archives, Oliver Ambrose Risdon Photograph Collection, PC 204_F.20_V.*

The Spoon Stage Line operated for many years between the towns of the county and into Willcox, Arizona. The line would transition to automobiles and small buses in later years. *Courtesy of the P.R.I.D.E. Society.*

1916, the hotel changed hands and names again when Thomas and May Simpson of Clifton purchased it.[85] Thomas worked for the railroad, and May operated the hotel. In 1922, room rates started at one dollar per night.[86] Thomas's sister Anna and her husband, Mike, owned and operated the Reardon Hotel in Clifton.

One of the lesser-known hotels in the valley was the Gardner Hotel, operated by Mrs. W.K. Gardner. It opened in 1908[87] and was sold to F.M. Crockett from Texas in 1912 for $2,000.[88] It was located across the street from the Bonnie Heather Inn.

The Bonnie Heather Inn was located where the current Riverfront Lounge stands. Bonnie's pool hall was a popular place over the years, and many social events were enjoyed there. The Bonnie now occupies a building near the Gila River bridge. The name of the business came from Wallace Duncan, a Scotchman who constructed the original building. The word *bonnie* means pretty, and the word *heather* refers to a flower in Scotland.[89]

Advertised as "the home of the best liquors and cigars"[90] in town, the Duncan Saloon was a favorite place to enjoy nightlife. Bart Tipton owned this establishment, and he was a keen businessman. He was engaged in farming, and the crops he owned supplied Duncan and Clifton merchants with fresh produce. Tipton was also involved with the mines of the Mayflower district.

Education and Sports

Duncan Valley was once home to numerous school districts, several of which consisted of one-room schoolhouses. The Day School, located near the Lunt farms, and the Neblett School in the Franklin area were examples of this. School warrants issued in June 1914 varied around the county; Duncan's was $5,109.74, Day's was $1,291.04, Franklin's was $1,812.13 and Sheldon's was

$998.43, compared to $42,275.67 for Clifton.[91] The Duncan-area districts were consolidated later that year.[92]

Duncan Grammar School was perched at the end of Main Street overlooking the town. The school was built in 1908. Classes for all grades were held here.[93] In 1953, the American Legion bought the building from the school district, as it was unused.[94] Soon the second floor was removed. It is now the home of American Legion McCullough-McNair Post 49.

Duncan High School was built in 1915 and based on plans of Lescher & Kibbey of Phoenix.[95] It was constructed by William S. Humphrey of Clifton for $25,450 using mottled pressed brick from El Paso, Texas.[96] The building was formally dedicated on April 1, 1916. Attendees included C.O. Case, state superintendent of schools; professors Foster of the University of Arizona and Irish of the Tempe Normal School; and J.W. Aker, the Greenlee County Schools superintendent. A special train from Clifton brought people to the event. Following the dedication, a track-and-field meet was held in front of the school. Competitions included the fifty-yard dash, shot put, mile race, running broad jump and a girls' basketball game.[97] On November 15, 1919, a fire started on the second

Sports teams from the Duncan Valley were always very competitive, as was this baseball team of mostly cousins from the Gale, Gilliland and Tippets families. *Gerald D. Hunt personal collection.*

Above: Duncan High School sits prominently overlooking the town in 1957. The architecture firm for this building also designed many structures in Clifton and Morenci after a name change to Lescher & Mahoney. *Robert A. Chilicky personal collection.*

Opposite, top: The Duncan Elementary School and gymnasium sustained severe damage during the 1972 flood and was razed soon after. *Courtesy of the Arizona Historical Society Library & Archives, Oliver Ambrose Risdon Photograph Collection, PC 204_F.19_H.*

Opposite, middle: Buses await schoolchildren outside the gymnasium and high school. *Robert A. Chilicky personal collection.*

Opposite, bottom: The schoolhouse in Franklin. *Courtesy of the Arizona Historical Society Library & Archives, Oliver Ambrose Risdon Photograph Collection, PC 204_F.21_C.*

floor, causing the roof to collapse. The flames quickly spread throughout the upper floor; in a short time, the bottom floor was ablaze.[98] For the next few years, classes were held in the Presbyterian Church, while the Methodist Church was used for the auditorium and study hall.[99] Finally, in 1921, contractors Cotey & Black of Clifton won the contract to rebuild the school for $45,830. Additionally, the firm purchased the $30,000 bond the school district had voted on in the spring of 1920.[100] In November 1921, the school started a newspaper, *Round Up*. Local businesses were eager to advertise in it, as the third annual Greenlee County Fair was to be held at the school that month.[101] The purchased ads gave the school much-needed revenue. In 1955, when Virden High School closed, twenty-nine

students started to attend Duncan High School. The state of New Mexico paid the Duncan School District $5,000 a year to cover transportation and education costs.[102]

Duncan Elementary School and its gymnasium were built in 1926 for $50,000.[103] The gym was home of the Duncan High School boys' basketball team, which won state championships from 1938 to 1940. This was an amazing accomplishment, as there was only one state tournament and Duncan competed against much larger schools. The teams were coached by Frank Brickey, who went on to coach at his alma mater, Arizona State Teachers College (Northern Arizona University), and later at the University of Utah. Al Fenn, Clifton Golden Gloves boxing manager and one-time *Copper Era* editor, was on the Benson High School team that lost to Duncan in the 1939 title game. In February 1939, legendary athlete Jim Thorpe spoke at a school assembly during his tour of Arizona.[104] The 1940 game against Tucson High School was a thriller, with All-State player Gene O'Dell making the winning basket in overtime. Duncan defeated Morenci in the semifinals, 26–24. Morenci had defeated Duncan in the previous two meetings during the regular season.[105] O'Dell was drafted in 1948 by the New York Knickerbockers.[106] It is worth mentioning that the Virden High School boys' basketball teams won New Mexico state championships in 1934 and 1944. The state also had only one tournament, and with a school population of less than sixty in 1934[107] and just thirty-five in 1944,[108] Virden competing and winning against much larger schools was no small feat.

A new gymnasium for Duncan schools was built next to the high school in 1949 at a cost of $170,000. Along with the athletic amenities, the building also had music classrooms and agricultural and manual training shops.[109] The building was formally dedicated on December 1, 1949, with two exhibition basketball games. First, the Arizona State College freshman team defeated Gila Junior College, 57–44. Then, Texas Western College outlasted Arizona State College, 67–61.[110] Many memorable teams have played here throughout the years. The high school girls' volleyball and the boys' and girls' basketball teams have won state championships. On the outdoor courts, the boy's and girl's tennis teams have won more than thirty team state titles and over fifty singles and doubles state championships.

School District Number 27 was in the Franklin area in early Greenlee County. At one time, the district was partly in New Mexico, because the town was close to the border and the population of the area was sparse.[111] The school here was built in 1912 with the help of Henry Hill of Clifton, who purchased the $2,500 bond needed for construction.[112] Contractor

L.P. Miller built the school using Portland cement blocks and materials from the Duncan Lumber Company. The Board of Directors of the Day School were so impressed with the structure that they planned a building of similar design.[113] The school was used until 1952, when Gene O'Dell bought the building and used the bricks for a home in New Mexico.[114] The great-grandfather of author Gerald D. Hunt, Hyrum Henry Tippets, donated the land for the school. He was trustee of the Neblett Water District and an advocate of education.[115]

Sheldon School District Number 32 was between York and Duncan. The rural school was typical, with children attending from the neighboring ranches. The school expenditure in January 1914 was $5.00, compared to $4,628.91 for the Clifton schools.[116] Like most schoolhouses, it served as a polling place during elections and was used as a meetinghouse for community business.

BRIDGES

Duncan is divided by the Gila River, causing issues during floods and high water. When the river rose, it made travel difficult if not impossible. For example, schoolchildren who lived on the north side of the river could not attend school on the south side. In 1903, a 600-foot pedestrian bridge with handrails was built to help with this problem at a cost of $600.[117] As the town grew, a larger bridge was needed. In 1912, the El Paso Bridge and Iron Company started construction on a steel bridge that could accommodate vehicle traffic.[118] Numerous construction and funding issues and floods caused the bridge to be not fully completed. Finally, in September 1915, the 1,500-foot-long bridge was completed,[119] however, in October 1916, a flood destroyed the entire span.[120] The bridge has been reconfigured several times throughout the years. Today, a modern span of 1,300 feet allows travelers safe passage over the river.

The long-awaited bridge over the Gila River near Three Way was completed in 1950 at a cost of $400,000.[121] The 726-foot bridge spanned the river on the new highway connecting Safford and Clifton. This highway replaced the dirt road known today as the Black Hills Back Country By-Way, making the trip considerably safer and faster. The café nearby was known as El Puente and was a popular destination for many years.

The concrete bridge over the Gila River on the Clifton–Solomonville road west of Guthrie was completed in 1918 for $60,200. It was originally

An early version of the bridge over the Gila River in Duncan. *Courtesy of the Greenlee County Historical Society.*

This bridge near Three Way was replaced in 2009, and the new structure crosses the Gila River just to the east of its former location. *Courtesy of the Greenlee County Historical Society.*

The bridge west of Guthrie has survived numerous floods, which is a testament to the outstanding engineering and craftsmanship of the builders. *Courtesy of the Greenlee County Historical Society.*

intended to be a steel bridge designed and built by the state, but material shortages caused by World War I meant a halt to the project. Local inmates built the road through this area, while the state hired the Topeka Bridge & Iron Company for the bridge construction. The job was completed at only about $200 over budget.[122]

Mining

The communities of the valley are not considered mining towns, but mining in the surrounding mountains has played an important role in their development and history. The Ash Peak area, about fifteen miles west of Duncan, was named for the numerous ash trees that grew along Ash Spring. It was an important mining district for many years and was the location of several mines owned by the Ash Peak Mining Company and other companies. An explosion in a mine owned by the Commerce Gold and Silver Mining Company on February 18, 1901, killed six miners and a stockholder from Massachusetts who was visiting the mine. Dozens more were injured, and the blast was heard and felt twenty miles away.[123] In 1906, the Ash Peak Mining Company built ore bins at

Above: Ash Peak along westbound Highway 70 in 1936. *Courtesy of the Arizona Historical Society Library & Archives, Oliver Ambrose Risdon Photograph Collection, PC 180_F.74_425.*

Left: Duncan office for the Twin Peaks Mining & Milling Company. *Courtesy of the Greenlee County Historical Society.*

Coronado Station along the Arizona & New Mexico Railway.[124] This enabled the company to ship ore to the Shannon Copper Company smelter in Clifton. In 1917, there were enough schoolchildren living in the area to justify the mining company's donation of a building and furniture for a school. Three women served on the school board.[125]

In the late 1800s, a ranger station was established at Ash Spring, and it was a frequent stopping place for people traveling by wagon to water their animals and spend the night. In later years, a service station, school, store, hotel, saloon and dance hall were built for the growing population. Nearby mining districts included Steeple Rock, Twin Peaks, Mayflower and East Camp. The mines were important producers of gold, silver, copper, zinc, lead and other minerals. The Carlisle District in New Mexico was a major contributor to the growth of Duncan. Many area residents worked there, so a stage line was established, initially by Apolonio Casados and then by W. Nunn.[126] Other mining companies operating in the area were the Duncan Gold Mining and Smelting Company, the Eclipse Mining Company, the Norman King Gold Mining Company and the Veda Mining Company.

Chinese nationals were an integral part of the workforce in the early days of the county. The Lesinsky brothers brought a group from San Francisco to work in the mines and in support services.[127] Many found work throughout the area and eventually established a camp for those working in the Carlisle mines. There was a group of toughs along the Gila River that locals called the Gila Monsters. They intended to overtake the camp. The mine got word of the plan, and before the river gang attacked, a mine official in a heavy Irish accent shouted, "Give 'em hell, boys!" The marauders were repelled, and they did not attempt to raid again.[128]

SMALLER COMMUNITIES

Three other important communities along the Gila River are Sheldon, York and Guthrie. The town of Sheldon grew around the station established by the Arizona & New Mexico Railway. The post office here was established on August 27, 1908 with John F. Holder as postmaster. It was discontinued on November 29, 1919.[129] Some say the town was named for New Mexico governor Lionel Sheldon, but it could have been named for a railroad engineer. York Station was established along the Arizona & New Mexico Railway as one of the stops where mining companies loaded their ore on the trains headed to the Clifton smelters. The name comes from rancher

Mine officials stop at a store in York before heading to a nearby mine. *Courtesy of the Greenlee County Historical Society.*

Guthrie served as an important transfer point between the Arizona & New Mexico Railway and the narrow-gauge Morenci Southern Railway. *Courtesy of the Greenlee County Historical Society.*

George R. York, who was also in the territorial legislature. He was killed near Doubtful Canyon on October 13, 1881.[130] York has the distinction of having the first post office in the Gila River Valley, established on January 16, 1882, with Lou M. Butler as postmaster. It was discontinued on July 9, 1883, and reestablished on May 9, 1911. It was then discontinued for good on February 28, 1920.[131]

Guthrie, about ten miles south of Clifton, emerged as an important community centered on the railroad. The post office was established on February 6, 1901, with Ellen J. Brown as postmaster, and was discontinued on August 15, 1922.[132] It was named for John Guthrie Smith, a director for the Arizona Copper Company. The town evolved because it was a gathering place for construction crews while building the Arizona & New Mexico Railway in 1883. Soon, a store and six saloons were built.[133] As families with school-age children settled in town, a school was authorized. The town had switch yards, homes, a depot, a post office and other businesses. It was somewhat remote, and there was only one road in and out of town that connected to the Clifton-Duncan Highway. Communications with the outside world was via telegraph and postal service until 1917, when telephone service was established.[134]

In August 1889, Carrie N. Hunt from Kansas was passing through Guthrie with her friend and fellow teacher Addie Adair on their way to Clifton. They accepted teaching positions in the Clifton School District and, while stopped at Guthrie Station, decided to send a letter home. They let their families know they were well and were excited about the upcoming school year. Their pay was eighty dollars a month, for nine months, and they were amazed that the school district was as big as four districts back in Kansas. Happily, they would not have more than twenty students each.[135]

CLIFTON, MORENCI AND METCALF

The Heart of Mining

The Metcalfe brothers had several mines in the Burro Mountains southwest of Silver City, New Mexico. They decided to sell the property to E.B. Ward of Detroit, Michigan. Ward had recently heard the reports of mountains of copper in eastern Arizona, and word quickly spread. He sent representatives into the San Francisco River area to prospect and report back to him on their findings. The Metcalfes organized a group to explore the findings and establish claims, but Ward asked them to go to the Burro Mountains to help finalize the sale of their mines. As they prepared to leave, a friend let them know that Ward planned to send his own prospectors to the Arizona site while the brothers and their crew were traveling to the Burro Mountains. They hastily loaded their pack animals and headed toward their property but then quickly diverted to the west and the San Francisco River. They would soon discover that in their rush to be the first to fully explore and claim any riches, they had put their group in great danger by omitting some critical supplies. The wild canyons and mountains contained risks, and making it even more daunting was the fact that Indians were killing soldiers, prospectors and settlers who dared enter the region.

Fortunately, the Metcalfes knew the route because they had been there in 1870, when they were serving in the army and chasing marauding Indians. Now, in 1872, they made the trip in four days and immediately went to work discovering and making claims on land that appeared to have rich mineralization. On the mountains above Chase Creek, a tributary to the "Frisco" river, they were able to establish claims on the

Longfellow, Metcalf and other ore bodies. Two days after the Metcalfes began work, the Ward party showed up. Imagine their surprise when they discovered that they had been beaten to the area and the Metcalfes were not where they thought they would be. In a short time, Ward's group established claims in the place that would eventually become the great mining town of Morenci, Arizona. These claims evolved into the Detroit Copper Mining Company. When the Metcalfes and associates finished their work, their supplies were getting low, so they began their return to Silver City. Robert Metcalfe asked one of his companions to shoot at a tree to test his marksmanship and assure them he could defend the group. The man got a puzzled look on his face and realized that Metcalfe didn't know they had not packed ammunition or powder.[136] One can only imagine the men's shock when they realized they had made the whole trip without the means to protect themselves. Their whole adventure had been courting disaster.

Town Descriptions

Clifton was founded in 1873[137] as the miners settled near the confluence of the San Francisco River and Chase Creek. Businessmen Henry and Charles Lesinsky owned several claims, and their success helped Clifton grow quickly as they expanded their mining and smelting operations. Experiencing limited smelting success with their first adobe furnaces, in 1874, the Longfellow Copper Mining Company moved its primitive smelter from the Rock House location on Chase Creek to a larger and more efficient smelter where Chase Creek emptied into the San Francisco River.[138] The Arizona Copper Company purchased the Longfellow group in 1882 and continued expanding and making improvements to the smelter and refining complex.[139] In 1902, the Shannon Copper Company built a smelter and concentrator on Cemetery Hill, now called Shannon Hill, to process ore from Metcalf. The first ore train was decorated with flags, and its arrival in Clifton was a cause of great celebration.[140] The Arizona Copper Company, headquartered in Scotland, built a new smelter in 1913. It was located two miles south of Clifton and replaced the Chase Creek facility.[141] It incorporated modern smelting techniques and improved the air quality in town. It is still a matter of debate if the town got its name from a man named Henry Clifton who came from the Prescott area in search of placer deposits, or from the numerous cliffs along the San Francisco River.

This early smelter in Clifton was near the location of the present-day Circle K. *Gerald D. Hunt personal collection.*

As the mines of the Copper Mountain Mining District were being developed in 1872, Captain Miles Joy led his surveying party into the area,[142] which soon became known as Joy's Camp. The river smelter site, about three miles south of Clifton along the San Francisco River, was known as Morenci.[143] This facility was operated by the Detroit Copper Company, led by William Church. The smelter was beset with smelting and ore shipping problems and was attacked by Indians. Church was even held at gunpoint and beaten by robbers, who forced him to empty the company safe. In early 1884, the company began to relocate its smelter and town closer to the mines. The February 2, 1884 *Arizona Weekly Citizen* reported that as the smelter was being moved from the river site and "there will be nothing left of the present town of Morenci, it is proposed to move the name up to the mines also, and the town up there will be called 'Morenci.'"[144] When the community was being settled, people lived in tents, so the area was known as *las carpas* to the Spanish-speaking population.[145]

The Great Depression brought about the closure of most of the mines, but in the 1930s, open-pit operations began and saved the company and towns, but not without consequence. The town of Morenci was always known to be sitting on a large body of low-grade ore. It was only a matter of time before the town had to move again. Housing was built in the Plantsite area in the 1940s; slowly, businesses, schools and churches were moved there so that mining operations had full access to the huge ore deposits. By the early 1980s, the old townsite no longer existed and everything had been moved to the townsite at Plantsite.

The origin of the town's name is still up for discussion. It has been speculated that it is named for Morenci, Michigan, as several men of the Detroit Copper Company had ties to that state. It has also been argued that the name comes from a girl Church saw in a show. He had connections to the Tombstone district through his brother, who was involved with the mines in that area. A young lady named Victoria Morenci was a member of a traveling musical comedy act performing there for several years.[146] One can only wonder if Church had seen her in a show and named the town in her honor.

Metcalf was a vibrant community nestled along Chase Creek Canyon and Coronado Gulch. The town had an elementary school and a large high school building, and the Arizona Copper Company had a store here. The company also operated three stores in Clifton and one each in Morenci, Longfellow and Coronado. The Shannon Copper Company had a store here as well, and in Clifton. On the south end of town was the BBB General

Site 2 (*left*) and Site 3 (*right*) of Plantsite in the late 1940s. *Robert A. Chilicky personal collection.*

Looking south along Chase Creek Canyon, the elementary school and Arizona Copper Company store are on the left, and the trestle across Coronado Gulch for the Shannon-Arizona Railway is on the right. *Courtesy of the Greenlee County Historical Society.*

Merchandise Store, White Owl Saloon and other buildings. The land these buildings were erected on was first owned by Jim Baldwin, who also owned a saloon in Clifton. Baldwin learned that a small parcel on the southern hillside of town was not owned by any of the copper companies, so he built his saloon there. The Arizona Copper Company owned the land adjacent to the saloon and tried for years to make him move. The company decided to re-survey their land and found the saloon property was overlapping theirs by three feet. The company demanded he move the building. Not giving in, Baldwin had carpenters cut three feet off the bottom floor but kept the top floor untouched. The company still complained, but he told them, "The land may belong to you, but you don't own the air!"[147]

It was densely populated, with houses close to one another. In some places, one could walk on the roofs and go house to house without setting foot on the ground. Mining activities went on around the clock, and large amounts of money flowed through Metcalf businesses and banks. Besides mining, people were drawn to Metcalf to view the spectacular mountains and scenery along the canyons. The railroads hauled trainloads of people on sightseeing trips.

Once the mine overtook the town, it did not relocate. During the 1930s, the town was vacated; only a few of the skeletal structures, walls and foundations remained. The impressive high school building remained as a symbol of the once proud town. It seemed out of place to travelers along Highway 666 as they looked up Coronado Gulch and saw the impressive building standing alone. The building was sold to a Clifton contractor for $1,000 in 1940, and he dismantled it.[148] The last business was a small store offering travelers a few items, but it was a far cry from the bustling town of just a few years before. It is a ghostless ghost town, in that Metcalf no longer exists and all the graves from the local cemetery were moved. Phelps Dodge hired a mortician from Ajo in 1950 to relocate all the graves to a location near Sacred Heart Cemetery. The last occupant to leave town was a goat rancher named Campos, who herded his flock down Chase Creek Canyon to Clifton,[149] thus ending what was once one of the largest towns in Graham and Greenlee Counties. There is no question of the origin of the town's name, but for some reason the brothers dropped the *e* from their name in naming the town.

Post Offices

The post office in Clifton was established in March 1875, with Charles Lezinsky as the first postmaster.[150] The post office near the railyard was built in 1910.[151] This section of town was a busy area, with the mine company general office and mercantile; various businesses, including the Clifton Ice Plant; and the train station. For many years, Tommy Sidebotham, a well-known Clifton law officer, stood on a stool in the middle of the intersection near here during mine shift changes. Many workers drove through this narrow section of road. Woe be to the driver who exceeded the fifteen-mile-per-hour speed limit and did not pay close attention to Sidebotham's hand signals and whistle. Rocks sometimes fell from the cliffs above, making driving hazardous and occasionally damaging buildings. Between 1917 and 1925, three major rockslides caused heavy damage to the post office building.[152] Luckily, it was vacant each time. William B. Kelly, who was postmaster from 1914 to 1918, became a state senator in the 1930s.[153] The post office was moved to its current location in 1957[154] and has plenty of parking spaces that are well off the street.

The first post office in Morenci was established on March 3, 1884, with George W. Davison as postmaster.[155] When the Morenci Club was built in 1902, it was moved there. In 1949, the shopping center was built, and the post office found a home in one of the wings.[156] This location shut down in September 1967, when the new post office in Plantsite was completed.[157]

The location of the Clifton Post Office made it convenient for people, but the building was right along the street, making it a dangerous spot during heavy traffic. *Courtesy of the Greenlee County Historical Society.*

Even though Metcalf was founded in the 1870s, the post office was not established until August 25, 1899, and was closed on May 15, 1936.[158] Sophia Shirley became the first postmaster, and she served until 1904, with several postmasters following her. She became postmaster again in 1922. Shirley was also a grade-school teacher in Clifton and Metcalf. She married Clark Farnsworth in 1913. After the post office closed, residents had to travel to Clifton for mail service.[159] Sophia was known as a kind-hearted person. Along with her postal duties, she helped deliver babies, assisted doctors during typhoid outbreaks and even built coffins. In the 1930s, as the town was closing, she prepared school lunches in her own kitchen.[160]

Entertainment, Social Life and Sports

Clifton's rich social life and entertainment opportunities compared favorably with much larger cities. There have been many company, school, church and civic organizations in the town throughout the years, but there was one group that was very unusual. It was common in the early days that the wives and daughters of the wealthier men would travel to the West Coast for the summer months, largely to escape the summer heat. The absence of the ladies left the men with more time on their hands than their spouses probably realized. A group called the Summer Widowers was established to encourage the men to get together socially. It was not a group with the intent to make money or do charity work, but rather for the gentlemen to have a good time together. During one meeting in 1905, it was found that the treasurer had thirty cents left over from the previous meeting, so he was fined one round of lemonade. The Clifton group was a leader in organizing men from other towns who asked for guidance to establish their own groups. Also, in 1905, some men from Tucson paid for the Clifton leadership to travel there to help them start up their organization. Groups from Bisbee and Douglas were also established under the guidance of the Clifton delegation. Graham County sheriff John Parks petitioned to join the Clifton group, as he was not a resident. After a discussion, he was allowed to join, but only after supplying the group with cigars. Another man gained membership after providing a gallon of ice cream.[161] The reports of the meetings were printed in the *Copper Era*, but some of the men did not want their names printed, as they feared their wives and daughters would hear about their fun and return early and put an end to it. In 1906, the editor of the newspaper printed a poem about the group, poking fun at them. The poem joked in part:

Tell them that the world is dreary,
and you're lone with them away;
If you tell them you're unhappy,
they will settle down and stay;
If you tell them you are happy
and play poker in the gloam;
You'll make a big mistake, for they
will come right home.[162]

The Morenci Club was a favorite place for residents to enjoy leisure time. The club offered many amenities, such as a bowling alley, billiards, snack bar, gymnasium, reading room, theatre, card room and large kitchen and adjoining space for special functions. Frequent dances were a popular activity. When the club was formally opened on April 28, 1902, noted geologist Waldemar Lindgren gave a speech entitled "The Geological Formation of the Clifton-Morenci District."[163] Club members could sit along the veranda, enjoying a cigar and conversation with friends while viewing the picturesque Morenci Canyon. In 1905, the club's gymnasium was the site of the first game for the University of Arizona men's basketball team. They played the Morenci YMCA in a tournament that also included the Bisbee YMCA.[164]

Next to the Morenci Club was one of the few flat spots in town to play baseball. Note the baselines laid out and the scoreboard on the fence at left. *Robert A. Chilicky personal collection.*

The copper companies throughout the Southwest sponsored baseball teams. Many of the players were company workers, while others were employed only as players. Games were well attended, and sometimes the railroads had special trains to transport fans between the towns. Pride was at stake, and so was money, as fans placed bets on their teams. A man named John Tortes "Chief" Myers, who went on to play for the New York Giants, played for the Arizona Copper Company team in the early 1900s. In a game against the Detroit Copper Company team on the field in South Clifton, Myers hit a game-winning home run. Fans were so excited that they collected $100 for the team. Two barrels of beer were bought at the Clifton Ice Plant, and the team and fans enjoyed a beer bust and food at Potter's Ranch north of Clifton.[165]

The Empire Theater opened on Chase Creek on August 29, 1908.[166] It featured first-class moving pictures along with piano entertainment by Mrs. A.A. Coleman. Miss Earle provided beautiful vocals. The theater gave two shows every evening for fifteen cents. To commemorate the grand opening, a souvenir prize was presented to a lucky patron. Children were also welcomed, as the theater awarded prizes to them as well.[167] Wilbur Wright brought a film of the famous plane *Flyer* to Clifton in 1909 and showed it here.[168] The theater hosted the third commencement exercises for Clifton High School in 1911. Sharlot Hall, territorial historian, addressed the graduates and crowd

58

Arizona Copper Company cricket team on the baseball field in South Clifton, December 1907. Shown here are General Manager Norman Carmichael (*standing, far left*) and Assistant Manager A.T. Thomson (*standing to Carmichael's left*). *Courtesy of the Greenlee County Historical Society.*

Looking west along Chase Creek. The tall building on the left above the Dunn & Loomis Drug Store is the Empire Theater. *Courtesy of the Greenlee County Historical Society.*

on the work of her office and recited a poem she wrote, "The Hero of the Smelter."[169] The museum in Prescott, Arizona, is named in her honor. The theater burned down in 1924.[170]

In 1912, the Jones Brothers Circus came to Clifton. The circus held a daily parade down Chase Creek. During one of these parades, an elephant frightened a delivery horse when it let out a bellow as it was trying to reach for some peanuts it saw in a store window. The driver of the wagon managed to calm the horse down, but then the circus band passed by, causing the horse to bolt. The horse ran down the street at full speed with the wagon in tow, scattering eggs, tomatoes and corn before the wagon finally overturned.[171] The circus also performed in Metcalf and at the Star Theater in Morenci.[172]

Good entertainment for the hardworking population was a priority for businessmen. The Princess Theater in Clifton, which opened in 1913, fit that requirement. Nationally renowned acts performed here, and motion pictures were shown. The venue also had a first-class confectionery.[173] During Fourth of July activities in 1935, local boxer Bob Ford fought Fred Goodall of Texas.[174] The building was damaged beyond repair during the 1983 flood and was demolished. Other theaters in Clifton over the years were the Armory, Lyric, Clifton Theater, Airdome, Royal, Martin and Prettyman's Opera House.

The tennis court was built as a part of the amenities offered to members of the Morenci Club. In 1914, lights were added because players complained

Dances, high school graduations, political rallies and boxing and wrestling matches were some of the events held at the Princess Theater. *Robert A. Chilicky personal collection.*

Morenci Club members enjoy a tennis match. *Courtesy of the Greenlee County Historical Society.*

about lack of playing time due to the high hills surrounding the town that blocked sunlight in the early evening.[175] At the high schools, Morenci has won eighteen boys' and girls' team championships and twenty-five singles and doubles state championships. Clifton has won eleven boys' and girls' team championships and twenty-four singles and doubles state championships.

The 1916 Labor Day celebration in Clifton was a grand event and was well attended by people from around the region. Thousands of people were in town for festivities, including bronco busting, a pie-eating contest, a wheelbarrow race, tug-of-war and a hard-rock drilling contest. There was a wrestling match at the Princess Theater between Al Wassem of St. Louis, the lightweight world champion, and Gus Eisel, the undefeated champion from Chicago. Many floats and bands highlighted the big parade from Chase Creek to South Clifton, with Arizona governor G.W.P. Hunt at the reviewing stand at the Reardon Hotel. Four dances were held in various places around town.[176]

On June 21, 1919, Arizona Copper Company manager Norman Carmichael hosted a garden party and dance for company employees returning from the war. A wide range of food, along with watermelon, ice cream and cake, were served. The centerpiece of the refreshment booth was a large punchbowl and stand made entirely from ice. It was decorated with colored lights and flowers that had been frozen into the rim. Decorations of Japanese lanterns, electric lights and flags of allied nations, as well as music provided by a brass band from Morenci, made for a memorable evening.[177] Carmichael wanted to give back to the community by hosting this large event.

A beautiful park was built next to the Morenci Club. Trees and shrubs were planted, creating a lovely scene. It was a favorite location for high school yearbook and personal photos and a place to enjoy spending time with friends. The large fountain and goldfish pond was an often-visited location. During Christmas season, the park was a winter wonderland, with a Christmas tree that everyone enjoyed. Santa Claus made his visit here and handed out to the children stockings filled with candy, toys, nuts and fruit.

In 1920, two relay races were held between boys from Clifton and Morenci High Schools. For the first race, the bridge into South Clifton was the finish line, with the starting point at Morenci Plaza. On February 28, Morenci won with a time of 25:10 to Clifton's 26:20. After the race, the awards ceremony and dinner was held at the high school auditorium, with girls from Clifton High School serving the group.[178] Then on November 20, the race went uphill from the bridge, ending at Morenci Plaza, with Clifton winning with a time of 32:15 to Morenci's 32:30. It was an exciting race, and the teams were tied going to the final runners, but Clifton's Bud Franz pulled ahead of his opponent for the win.[179] The bridge, completed in 1918, was constructed in four sections and capped by an arch. Each section was independent, with the idea that the entire bridge would not be destroyed in a flood. Near the end of construction, City Marshal John Young wanted to be the first person to use the bridge, so when workers were not looking, he drove his car across the span.[180]

An item of interest in the local area is the hot springs in the San Francisco and Gila Rivers. In the early days of Clifton, a local barber understood the mineral properties of the river and, probably more importantly, understood the commercial opportunity it offered. He constructed a crude bathhouse on the banks of the river near the rail yard. It had two tubs. For twenty-five cents, customers had the choice of a tub with hot water or one with warm water.[181] Years later, the Clifton Mineral Hot Springs Bath House was built in 1928, and a new era of tourism was on the horizon. The Coronado Trail had recently been completed, and city leaders were optimistic that travelers would soon be flooding into town. The bathhouse took advantage of the hot springs from the San Francisco River that flowed just yards from it. The building was dedicated on August 11, 1928, with Arizona congressman Lewis W. Douglas, grandson of former Phelps Dodge president Dr. James Douglas, giving the dedication speech. Various swimming, diving and racing events were held at the swimming pool next door, along with a bathing-suit contest. Copies of the June 18, June 20 and August 8 *Arizona Republican* newspaper describing the venue's construction, along with copies of the *Copper Era*, were

This concrete bridge spanning the San Francisco River was distinct in design. *Courtesy of the Greenlee County Historical Society.*

Construction of the Clifton Mineral Hot Springs Bath House. *Courtesy of the Greenlee County Historical Society.*

Promotional photo for the grand opening of the Martin Theatre in 1939. *Courtesy of the Greenlee County Historical Society.*

placed in a copper box in a cornerstone time capsule.[182] Also, a copper plate was placed on the outside of the building with the inscription, "The Clifton Mineral Hot Springs 1928."[183]

In continued efforts to improve the town, the city park on Clifton's Eastside was completed in 1930.[184] In this area once stood saloons, restaurants and brothels, so the beautification of Eastside was welcomed. Other improvements were sidewalks and trees lining the street. Along with the recently completed Mineral Hot Springs and Bathhouse and a city swimming pool, the park greatly enhanced recreational choices for the townspeople. The park gazebo was where Santa gave children Christmas stockings.

The Martin Theatre in Clifton opened for business in 1939. The company of McCormick and Nace owned the theater, along with the Royal Theatre in Morenci. Jean Rascoe and June Potter were the first ushers.[185] In January 1958, during a wave of youth and gang violence in Clifton and Morenci, the seats of the theater were slashed.[186] In later years, the building became a funeral home. Sadly, it was severely damaged during the 1983 flood and was demolished.

The world-famous Harlem Globetrotters traveled to Clifton in 1948 as a part of their tour of the Southwest. They were enjoying an eighty-nine-game win streak. Their opponent was a team from Duncan. This team, sponsored by Glen Axton's Gas and Stove Company, was considered the best in the Arizona Independent League. The game was on February 14 at

The pool in Morenci offered a great recreational location where generations of residents learned to swim, and the high school used it for physical education classes. *Courtesy of Tom Powers and the Morenci Lion's Club.*

the Clifton High School gymnasium and was played in front of a capacity crowd. The Globetrotters did not disappoint, with their usual antics and great basketball trick shots, but they soon realized the Duncan team meant business. The game ended up being a serious contest, with Duncan winning, 49–47. Gerald Jones had nineteen points and Gene O'Dell had thirteen to lead the Duncan team, while Cleo Johnson scored eighteen points to lead the Globetrotters.[187]

Hot summer days and nights were enjoyed by many people at the Morenci pool. It was built near the ruins of Arizona Copper Company's Concentrator Number 6, commonly known as "el molino." A favorite activity over the years was the free coin dive during Fourth of July celebrations. When the pool opened on September 10, 1953, an estimated six hundred children attended.[188] Local bands also played here on summer nights for teen dances. County historian Don Lunt helped to construct this pool. It was his first job when he returned from the Korean War.[189]

The Coronado Inn at the old train station in Clifton was a popular entertainment destination for many years. It had a bar and restaurant where excellent lunches and dinners were served. Various groups used the large ballroom on the second floor for functions and meetings. It was a popular place for dances. Author Gerald D. Hunt's band played for several wedding dances here in the 1960s.

Hotels

In the early days of Clifton, before hotels were built, Jack Abraham erected a tent near the base of the mountain on the east side of the San Francisco River. It had cots separated by sheets of cheesecloth. It was known as "telephone row," as conversations could be heard from one end to the other.[190] Abraham soon built the Clifton Hotel on the location of the tent and managed it with his wife, Martha. Not long after, more hotels were built, including the United States Hotel, the Grand Hotel and the Central Hotel, all on the Eastside. Later, a lesser-known hotel was established on Chase Creek called, aptly enough, the Chase Creek Hotel. It was in the old Royal Theatre building.[191]

Jack's brother Sam and Sam's wife, Laura, purchased the hotel from him. A double porch and sidewalk were added in 1909,[192] enhancing the appearance and guest satisfaction. Laura was one of the first people to own a car in Clifton. In 1910, while traveling between Metcalf and Clifton, she was arrested for speeding. Sam paid the fine in gold.[193] In 1932, the hotel was destroyed by a fire of unknown origin that started at night. Guests on the upper floors threw their mattresses out the windows to jump onto, and others climbed down the porch supports at the front of the building.[194]

Located on the Eastside, sections of the foundation for the Clifton Hotel are still visible today. *Courtesy of the Greenlee County Historical Society.*

The original section of the Central Hotel was the north side; in 1893, the addition on the south side was added. Hotel rooms were in high demand, so in 1901, owner George "Judge" Hormeyer had the second floor built, adding fifteen rooms. Hormeyer died in 1901, and his wife, Julia, continued operating the hotel. She married the contractor who worked on the hotel, W.A. Pitt, in 1903. When Clifton became incorporated in 1909, town offices were housed here until 1920.[195] After years of neglect and sustaining heavy damage in the 1972 and 1983 floods, the hotel has been fully restored and is in operation today as the Clifton Hotel.

Hotel Morenci, built in 1902, was recognized as one of the premier hotels in Arizona. The interior was lavishly furnished and designed. Guests enjoyed the lounging room, with its large, beautiful fireplace constructed of cobblestones.[196] In 1920, the hotel secured the services of William G. Bandee, a prominent French chef. He served in the French army during the Argonne campaign in World War I and was wounded three times and gassed. Before he was in the army, he was chef for a General Anderson of the U.S. Army.[197]

For many years, the Longfellow Inn in Morenci was a favorite place to have dinner or get a cold beer. It was also a popular place to hold church, school and town functions. The friendly staff held the needs of the customers in high priority. The lower level had horse stables in the early days, and they were built into the hillside. In 1907, as the finishing touches were being completed on the outside, contractor W.A. Pitt fell off the scaffold to the

The Central Hotel, at left, was built in the early 1890s as a one-story building using bricks made from slag. *Robert A. Chilicky personal collection.*

The Hotel Morenci was designed by the firm Trost & Rust from Tucson. *Courtesy of the Greenlee County Historical Society.*

The Longfellow Inn was first managed by the Arizona Copper Company, then later by Phelps Dodge. *Gerald D. Hunt personal collection.*

In the early days, the Reardon Hotel also had a balcony and porch on the back side, giving guests a great view of Shannon Hill and the San Francisco River. *Robert A. Chilicky personal collection.*

ground. He broke his left shoulder and right arm below the elbow. He was also temporarily paralyzed.[198] Pitt constructed many other buildings in Morenci and Clifton.

The Reardon Hotel in Clifton was built in 1913 by local contractor J.L. Morris, based on the plans of D.K. Mason, assistant chief Engineer of the Arizona & New Mexico Railway.[199] The hotel was owned and operated by Michael and Anna Reardon. Michael worked for the railroad, while Anna operated the hotel, just as her brother and sister-in-law Thomas and May Simpson did for the Simpson Hotel in Duncan. In January 1914, a fire in the kitchen was quickly extinguished before spreading and causing more damage.[200] The hotel had the contract to provide meals for prisoners in the Clifton jail at twenty cents a meal.[201] Michael died in 1927 after falling off a Southern Pacific freight car as the train was stopped in Franklin.[202] The refurbished Reardon still provides comfortable rooms for travelers visiting the area.

Religion

Many officials of the Arizona Copper Company were Presbyterian. The congregation had a small building in North Clifton for church services, but a more fitting building was needed. In 1899, the Presbyterian church building at Tombstone was dismantled and rebuilt in North Clifton.[203] Although it was arranged that Clifton would acquire the building, residents from Tombstone later claimed it was stolen from them.[204] The building met the local congregation's needs for only a short time. In 1902, the Arizona Copper Company donated land and $500 for a new building.[205] By 1917, however, the church population had grown considerably, so a larger building was in order. A site on the Eastside was selected as a more central location. Construction began in 1918 by J.L. Westerman of El Paso, Texas. The main floor had an auditorium, and the basement had two classrooms, a dining room with a kitchen, a pantry, storage rooms and a room for organ machinery. The building was heated with hot water. Formal dedication services took place on Easter Sunday in 1920, with the Reverend George Logie of Phoenix presiding. By 1975, the building no longer met the needs of the people, so the congregation moved into a larger building in Morenci. For a time, it served as a Masonic Lodge.[206]

The Presbyterian church building in Clifton is still in use today as a bed-and-breakfast called the Blue Door Sanctuary. *Courtesy of the Greenlee County Historical Society.*

The Morenci Presbyterian Church was near the base of Copper Mountain and above the Detroit Copper Company Store. *Courtesy of the Greenlee County Historical Society.*

A petition to establish the Morenci Presbyterian Church was circulated in May 1899,[207] and the church opened on March 4, 1900.[208] In the 1940s, the church sponsored an all-church picnic at Potter's Ranch, which is north of Clifton along the San Francisco River. Today, the bell of this church is in the bell tower of the Shepherd of the Hills Presbyterian Church in Morenci, along with the bells from the Metcalf and Clifton Presbyterian churches.[209]

The Catholic community was under the Archdiocese of Tucson in the early days. The priest would travel from the Solomonville parish to provide services to Clifton, Morenci and at Saint Peter's in Metcalf. The first church building was established in North Clifton in 1889 but was washed away in the 1891 flood. Another church was soon built on Chase Creek near the present-day Cascarelli Building, but it burned down only a few months later. A third building was constructed nearby but was destroyed in the 1905 flood. Later that year, a wood-frame building was erected on the site of the present-day church. Over the years, the congregation grew, and the church became too small.[210] Between February 1, 1916, and January 31, 1917, the current rock church of Sacred Heart was built around the wood structure. On March 11, 1917, the church was officially dedicated, and six hundred members received confirmation during the weeklong celebration.[211]

Sacred Heart Catholic Church on Chase Creek has been a place of worship and sanctuary for generations of parishioners. *Courtesy of the Greenlee County Historical Society.*

Saint Michael's Catholic Church (*lower right*) on Shannon Hill was next to the cemetery. This church had a dirt floor. *Robert A. Chilicky personal collection.*

From baptisms and weddings to funerals and Sunday Mass, meeting the needs of the Catholic community was a high priority of the priest at Holy Cross. *Courtesy of the Greenlee County Historical Society.*

Holy Cross was on AC Hill in Morenci, overlooking the entire town. The church was dynamited several times in 1913, when anarchists tried to kill the priest. Clifton architect Duncan McNeil redesigned the damaged building.[212] In 1971, when the church was torn down, the windows, which were imported from Spain in 1917,[213] were removed and installed in the current Holy Cross church at the new townsite.[214]

Law(lessness) and Order

The towns in the early days were just as wild and dangerous as the more famous mining camps of the West. Shootings and murders were frequent, and many saloons and brothels lined the streets, creating a dangerous combination. One of the more famous gunfights in the district happened in Morenci on December 21, 1895. Around midnight, several men attempted to rob a general store in Morenci's notorious Hell's Half Acre. Paul Becker worked at the store, and the men held him at knife and gunpoint and tried to get him to open the safe while robbing him of fifty dollars. Becker fought them off and injured them but was stabbed several times. The robbers got away but left a trail of blood up a nearby hill. With the knife still in his back, Becker stumbled to

Law enforcement officers, including Tim Nardelli (*far left*) and Judge Theodore Shirley (*second from right*), are seen in Metcalf, 1907. *Robert A. Chilicky personal collection.*

Pablo Salcido's saloon, where several law enforcement officials were enjoying the evening. They pulled the knife from Becker's back and called for a doctor. Salcido was a popular saloon owner and the former Graham County recorder. The next morning, law enforcement officials followed the trail of blood up a hill about one hundred yards from the store. As they approached the house where the trail ended, the occupants emerged with guns drawn, and a gun battle ensued. The sheriff called for help as his men were pinned down. Salcido started up the hill to assist but was struck by a bullet to his forehead. When the smoke cleared, Augustine Chacón, the ringleader and a well-known horse thief, was taken into custody and two of his companions lay dead.[215] Chacón was tried and convicted of the murder of Salcido and sentenced to hang. While awaiting execution in Solomonville, he escaped and went on the run for several years until he was captured in Sonora, Mexico, in September 1902.[216] He was hanged in Solomonville on November 21, 1902.[217]

The first Clifton jail was created in 1881 from a small cave that had been used by Indians. A man named Margarito Varela was hired to make the area bigger by blasting the rock and installing an iron gate on each cell and main entrance. The story goes that when he completed the jail, he celebrated too much at a local saloon and became its first inmate.[218] The jail was of medieval appearance, and at one time, thirty-one inmates were stuffed into the cells that normally held up to twenty-four prisoners. Inmates spent their time in various activities, such as playing cards, sleeping or scratching images such as President Teddy Roosevelt or William Shakespeare into the rock walls. No restroom facilities were available, so the stench must have been overwhelming. Floods were always a concern, as the cells easily filled with water and mud. Such was the case during the flood of 1891. The raging river rose in one night, and the town was devastated. Sheriff John Hovey was on the opposite side of the river and realized an inmate named Germain Turtelott, who was known as "Friday," was trapped in his cell. Hovey could not get across, so he fashioned a huge sign that read, "Get Friday out of the balliwax." Men on the other side rushed to the jail and tried to open the door but could not. There was one opening in the rock for ventilation, but it was too small for Friday to fit through. They resorted to blasting another opening into the rock large enough to pull him through. The water was to Friday's waist, and he was injured from the blasting. As a result of Friday's misfortunes, the hole created to rescue him benefited future inmates, as the opening provided additional light and ventilation.[219] Morenci and Metcalf had jails built from abandoned mine tunnels. In later years, Clifton civic leaders recognized that the Cliff Jail could be a tourist attraction. In 1929, lights were installed inside and upgrades at the entrance were built to make

Margarito Valera stands next to Cliff Jail. Note that the air hole at upper right is several feet above the ground, whereas today it is at ground level. *Courtesy of the Greenlee County Historical Society.*

it safe for visitors.[220] This entire section of Clifton has been filled with several feet of tailings. As a result, the jail is now accessed by going down a set of stairs. It is an interesting location and gives a glimpse into territorial justice.

As in many towns of the West, sometimes the outlaws ran the town. Such is the case of James "Kid" Louis and his gang of about thirty men. They committed crimes during the day and drank in the local saloons at night, not fearing capture. The townsfolk knew them, as did local law enforcement and the judge. Louis and his men were arrested from time to time, but no judge—and certainly no jury—would convict them for fear for their own lives. His time to be held accountable would come quickly. The gang robbed William Church in broad daylight, and that night they celebrated. Sometime during the night, a girl who lived with Louis was shot during an argument. The Arizona Copper Company doctor was called to help but was out on another call. Another doctor was called, but the girl succumbed to her wounds. Louis vowed to kill the company doctor. The next day, James Colquhoun was arranging for the doctor to leave town, but western justice stepped in. A rancher who recently had cattle stolen by Louis and his men organized a posse to find the gang. As they neared the mouth of Ward Canyon near the San Francisco River, they came upon Louis and two of his men. The posse surrounded the outlaws and shot them from their saddles.[221]

The community of New Town had its own share of lawlessness. Shootings and murders were common, and the music and drunkenness resonating from the numerous saloons and brothels echoed through Morenci Canyon. In 1911, an argument between Constable Len Scott and Deputy Sheriff George Johnson broke out as the men were drinking in a saloon. The fight spilled out onto the street, and both men fired one shot, each missing badly. Then they took deliberate aim and fired simultaneously, hitting each other in the forehead. They were only about four feet apart, and the results were fatal. Johnson died instantly, while Scott suffered for about forty-five minutes.[222] The bad feelings between the two had been brewing for some time, ending with deadly results.

A high-profile murder trial was held in Clifton in 1918. On February 10, brothers Tom and John Power and family friend Tom Sisson were involved in a shootout with Graham County law officers at the Power family cabin in the Galiuro Mountains near Klondyke. The officers were serving a warrant on the brothers for evading the draft. Sheriff Robert F. McBride and Deputies Martin R. Kempton and Thomas K. Wootan were killed, and the Power brothers and Sisson were injured but escaped.[223] The three men went to Mexico, and the largest manhunt in Arizona history ensued. The

When the jail section of the Clifton Town Hall did not have inmates, the firemen used the cells as sleeping quarters. *Courtesy of the Greenlee County Historical Society.*

men were captured by the Third Squadron, Nineteenth U.S. Cavalry, based out of Hachita, New Mexico. When they were taken into custody, the men were in bad physical and mental shape. John suffered an eye injury during the shootout, and due to lack of treatment, it had maggots.[224] Greenlee County law officers Robert Stewart of Duncan and Arthur Slaughter of Clifton were in the group that brought the men back about a month after the shootout.[225] The defense asked for a change of venue from Graham County. The trial was moved to Clifton,[226] where the men were found guilty and sentenced to life in prison.

The Town Hall on Clifton's Eastside was completed in 1920. The architect was Duncan McNeil of Clifton, and it was built by the local contracting firm Cotey & Black at the expense of $15,000. It had offices for the mayor, clerk, city engineer, marshal and fire department, as well as a council chamber. The building had electric lights, steam heating and fireproof vaults for records. The jail annex had showers and other sanitary arrangements.[227] In 2014, as the building was being refurbished, workers found that the original color of the door for the fire engines was brilliant gold. They also found many rodent and bird nests in the upper crawl space and signs a mountain lion had once lived there, as they also found numerous half-eaten carcasses, including one of a javelina.[228]

Schoolhouses

Over the years, there have been more than thirty buildings in Clifton, Morenci and the Metcalf area where generations of children have received an education. Some have been one-room buildings such as the first school in Clifton, which was near the mouth of Ward Canyon at the San Francisco River; the small adobe building on the Eastside near the front of the current Clifton Hotel; the building near the Arizona Copper Company General Office; and the small school buildings at the camps of Coronado and Shannon in the mountains around Metcalf. The East Plantsite School was renamed Modoc, and the name of the Plantsite School between Sites 1 and 2 was changed to Longfellow in 1969.[229] Schools were segregated in the early days, with the Mexican School near Holy Cross in Morenci[230] and the Colored School on Chase Creek in Clifton.[231]

The public school in Morenci was a fine addition to the town. It was constructed by W.A. Pitt of Clifton. The school was dedicated on November 20, 1901, with an open-air ceremony in the schoolyard. President James Douglas of the Detroit Copper Company gave a speech about the change of the town from a group of tents on the hillside to the growing community it had become. He charged the citizens and school officials "to build up the camp in the higher and better ways of straight thinking and straight living."[232] A second floor was added between July and September 1907.[233]

North Clifton was a comfortable section of town for families. The homes in the early days were primarily for mining company managers. The North Clifton School was built in 1902 and burned down in 1942.[234] It was an excellent school for the children. W.A. Pitt constructed the school, which was entirely funded by the Arizona Copper Company. Behind the school was a large playground with access to the river. Watchful eyes of teachers were needed to keep playful children corralled and away from the river.

The South Clifton School was completed in 1908. The gentleman in charge of the contracting firm left town prior to its completion. He also left other construction projects around town unfinished. He was last seen in Duncan playing poker and squandering the last of his money.[235] The second floor was not complete when school started, and the Shannon Copper Company funded its completion.[236] School officials from the Latter-day Saints Academy (now Eastern Arizona College) in Thatcher, Arizona, came to Clifton to view the school and were so impressed that they patterned the main building of the academy after it.[237] When Laugharn Elementary School was completed in 1954, this old school was torn down

PUBLIC SCHOOL BUILDING—MORENCI.

The Morenci Public School was known as the Red Brick School, then later Longfellow.
Robert A. Chilicky personal collection.

by a contractor from Safford, Arizona, who was interested in the massive ceiling beams.[238]

Clifton High School was built in South Clifton in 1912. After the first high school building was damaged beyond repair during the January 1905 flood, classes were held in a variety of places, including the Santa Teresa building, South Clifton School and even in a large tent that was in the location of Maud's Café.[239] In 1941, the band room building behind the school was erected by students in the vocational shop classes.[240] In 1962, the school was repaired and improved with such items as automatic refrigerated water fountains and new exterior paint. The inside stairs were reinforced, and slip-proof aluminum treads were attached on each step. Additionally, new windows were installed, and the roof and furnace stack were repaired.[241] The building was torn down in 1978,[242] and the space is now occupied by the public library, which was built here after the 1983 flood. The band room building was purchased by Mike Fuller in 1976, and he remodeled the lower

The school in North Clifton was also known as the Colquhoun School, since its construction was entirely funded by the Arizona Copper Company. *Courtesy of the Greenlee County Historical Society.*

The South Clifton School was along Leonard Avenue and at the end of Third Street. *Robert A. Chilicky personal collection.*

Local construction firm Vandercook & Black built Clifton High School in 1912. *Courtesy of the Greenlee County Historical Society.*

level to a three-bedroom residence and shop. He rented the upper floor for groups needing a space for recitals and dance lessons.[243] Today, it continues to be used as apartment residences.

Liem Elementary School in Clifton was named for Henry A. Liem, a longtime Clifton schools superintendent. He came to Clifton in 1925 and was superintendent from 1928 to 1945. During the Great Depression, he secured money from the Works Progress Administration (WPA) to improve school facilities. With the help of the government money, Clifton Recreational Park was built in 1936[244] and dedicated as Stanton Stadium in 1937.[245] He was criticized for spending money on school districts that were losing students almost daily as families left town due to lack of work. His vision was realized when families flooded into town in the 1930s as open-pit operations began.[246] Liem School was on the corner of Laine Boulevard and Fourth Street in South Clifton and was damaged beyond repair during the 1983 flood.

In 1921, a large high school was built in Morenci. It had six floors, each with a ground-level entrance, and a spiral fire escape. It was dismantled in 1950. A new Morenci High School was completed in August 1949 at a cost of $741,000. Nine pastel colors for the classrooms were selected based on a book published by the St. Paul, Minnesota public schools, outlining exposure factors, size and room purpose to determine which colors to use.[247] The new gymnasium was officially dedicated in December 1949 with a basketball

Morenci High School was built on the site of the Detroit Copper Company smelter and machine shop. Each of the three stories had a ground entrance. *Robert A. Chilicky personal collection.*

game between Arizona State College and Texas Western College.[248] In 1954, a section was completed on the second floor next to the gymnasium adding four classrooms. In 1955, a beautiful auditorium was built on the left side of the structure. The school was well built, with reinforced concrete throughout. When Morenci was being dismantled, the building was buried beneath tons of waste rock and dirt after caving in the roof. The plush seats from the auditorium were taken out and installed in the new high school gymnasium in Plantsite in 1982.[249]

MINING AND SMELTING

The great open pit of the Morenci mine was, and still is, an awe-inspiring sight, astounding visitors with its enormous size. Before open-pit operations started in the late 1930s, Phelps Dodge was in financial distress. One of the major factors that saved the company was the decision to fully expose the massive Clay ore body through open-pit mining. The Clay Mine had been worked underground for many years, but the open-pit technique enabled miners to increase tonnage and productivity. A small hill on the southeast rim of the pit known as Dispatch Hill had a mine observation point.

Daily dynamite blasts chewed into the mountainsides as the benches of the pit were created. Children recall the afternoon blasts that shook the school buildings. Each level had rail lines for trains that hauled ore and waste rock. The train would dump waste rock into the canyons and haul ore to the mill crusher to begin the refining process. The pit was ever-changing, and maintaining the rail lines took constant work by track crews. The work of the numerous churn drills, trains, shovels, bulldozers, trucks and explosive crews was ongoing, day and night, through good weather and bad. The round-the-clock operation continues today.

In the early days, mining was exclusively underground, which was very complex. One of the more important materials used in the mines was the lumber needed to support the miles of tunnels that honeycombed the mountains. The support beams in the underground mines needed constant repair and replacement due to cave-ins, mine blasts and regular wear and tear. The lumber yard of the Detroit Copper Company was a busy place, as timber was commonly treated there with creosote and a zinc chloride solution that helped slow the decay process. The shopping center was built on this site in 1949.[250]

Mules, horses and burros were important in the day-to-day activities in the mines and communities. The rough and mountainous terrain necessitated their use. The mules are hardy, sure-footed animals capable of carrying heavy loads and working long hours. They worked countless days and hours in the underground mines, pulling ore cars and supplies. Occasionally, the animals were brought from the underground corrals to the surface. They had to be blindfolded and brought out at night so they would not go blind after working lengthy periods in the dark tunnels. They were also used for domestic and commercial use for delivery of water, groceries, furniture and firewood. Some people kept them as pets when they were relieved of their service. The mining companies held these animals in high regard and paid a high price for them. The Shannon Copper Company, for example, put an ad in the *Copper Era* in 1909 when a mule went missing. The company offered $25 (roughly $700 in today's money) for its safe return.[251]

Many underground mines were serviced by the inclines. Remnants of these inclines were still visible into the 1990s, long after the mines had shut down. The Queen Incline plunged down Queen Hill to the ore bins along Chase Creek. The Eagle and Fairplay Inclines came down Copper Mountain into Morenci. The King Incline was in King Gulch, and its rail line connected at the top of the Metcalf Incline. The Shannon Incline came down into Chase

MORENCI OPEN PIT MINE
MARCH 1938

Top: Early work along Ryerson Gulch in developing the open pit, March 1938. *Courtesy of the Greenlee County Historical Society.*

Bottom: Three ore cars are being pulled up the Longfellow Incline for transport to the Arizona Copper Company Concentrator Number 6 in Morenci. *Robert A. Chilicky personal collection.*

Creek north of Metcalf, and its ore was sent to the smelter on Shannon Hill in Clifton. The Wilson Incline was next to the Metcalf Incline. On July 28, 1907, miners for the Shannon Copper Company rode an empty ore car up the Metcalf Incline without permission. They were late for work and tried saving time by using the incline. The cable broke about 300 feet up, sending the car careening back down the mountainside, killing two and injuring six. One of the men killed was thrown 150 feet across Chase Creek; the other died at the hospital in Clifton.[252]

Looking north along Chase Creek Canyon, this train is near the ore bins for the Queen Incline. *Courtesy of the Greenlee County Historical Society.*

The Longfellow Incline was built in the 1870s and was the first of the nine inclines constructed to service the mines near Morenci. Ore cars were lowered by cable to the ore bins along Chase Creek, then trains took the ore to the mill and smelter. Along with mine activity, this incline served a special purpose in November 1909. William Jennings Bryan came to Clifton and delivered his famous "Prince of Peace" speech at the Clifton Armory. He then traveled up Chase Creek Canyon on the Coronado Railroad and toured Metcalf. At the Longfellow Incline, he boarded a special cable ore car and rode to the top, where he was met by Detroit Copper Company officials and a brass band. Bryan had dinner and stayed at Hotel Morenci. The next day, he rode the impressive underground Humboldt Electric Railway through Copper Mountain.[253] This ore haulage and transportation system was a world-renowned mine engineering accomplishment.

The Coronado Incline was said to be the longest in the world at over 3,200 feet. It connected the extensive mines on Coronado Mountain to Metcalf. Work on the inclines demanded strong cables and skilled hoist operators and crewmen, but accidents did occur. In August 1913, the drawbar on two ore cars broke at the top of the incline, sending the cars careening down the mountain. One car was loaded with twelve tons of ore, while another carried seventeen people. Eight people managed to jump out of the car at

The Coronado Incline is rising to the left, while the Humboldt Electric Railway connects from the side. *Courtesy of the Greenlee County Historical Society.*

the top and suffered various minor injuries, but nine persons met a horrific death. Body parts were scattered along the line. The superintendent of the Coronado Mine was one of the injured.[254] The little community at the top of the mountain was also named Coronado and had housing, a store and a school. Its post office operated between August 21, 1912, and November 30, 1919, with Samuel F. Lanford as postmaster. Dan J. Grant, an early miner, named the mountain Coronado.[255]

The reduction works of the Arizona Copper Company in Clifton was at a prime location, at the confluence of Chase Creek and the San Francisco River. Although the site was roughly ten miles from the farthest mines above Metcalf, the Coronado Railroad easily transported the ore to this location for processing. The facility took advantage of the San Francisco River, which provided waterpower via a flume from a dam upriver near Limestone Canyon. Trains transporting ore passed above the acid-leaching plant on their way to the ore bins. The first locomotive for the Arizona Copper Company was nicknamed "Emma." After it was retired in 1893, the engine was salvaged and used as an air compressor at the acid works.[256] In 1913, the Detroit Copper Company purchased the properties of the New England &

This view of the Arizona Copper Company smelter complex is from across the San Francisco River. Note the road coming down the mountain into Clifton. *Robert A. Chilicky personal collection.*

Clifton Copper Company and the Standard Mines Copper Company. When the smelter facility in Clifton was shutting down that same year, there was a rumor that the Detroit Copper Company was going to buy it to process ore from its mines. Arizona Copper Company general manager Norman Carmichael quickly put the rumor to rest, saying there was "positively nothing in it."[257]

This facility closed on January 1, 1914. To make the occasion momentous, a large amount of dynamite was placed into the converter and molten ore poured in. The explosion echoed throughout town. Later, due to the amount of copper in the soil, all the dirt at this location was removed to a depth of five feet and re-smelted at the new facility south of town.[258] Many of the buildings at the smelter complex had hand-cut slate roofing shingles imported from Scotland.[259]

The smelter facility south of Clifton was "blown in" on August 27, 1913,[260] although it was not completed until early 1914. After the December 1906 flood, when the company works in town was damaged, the Arizona Copper Company looked to this area as a safe place away from floods. The $3 million facility was very efficient, and the modern equipment greatly improved smelting techniques. The air quality in Clifton greatly improved when the new smelter facility was built away from the center of town. Cool air during the winter months frequently creates particularly bad air pollution. Air currents and atmospheric pressure often did not allow the sulfurous smelter smoke to rise, causing horrible living and working conditions. Using the

The Detroit Copper Company concentrator overlooking Ryerson Gulch. *Courtesy of the Greenlee County Historical Society.*

tracks of the Arizona & New Mexico Railway, a special Coronado Railroad train from Clifton provided workers transportation to and from work. The smelter stack was demolished in 1997.[261]

In operation from 1900 to 1921, the West Yankie Concentrator of the Detroit Copper Company in Ryerson Gulch northeast of Morenci was built to handle the low-grade ore being mined. Water for this facility was piped six miles from the San Francisco River. At the time it was built, it was the largest mill in Arizona.[262] Trains from the hoist area went through the Montezuma Tunnel and passed through Copper Mountain to the smelter in Morenci. The remnants of Queen City, one of the little-known camps of the district, sat atop the ridge across Ryerson Gulch. Sam Abraham co-owned a saloon here. It was known as a rough and rowdy community.[263]

The silver and gold mines of the Stargo Mines Incorporated were in Apache Gulch and Silver Basin near Morenci. They were acquired by Phelps Dodge in 1931. These mines were one of the last properties bought by the company during its ten-year takeover of all the major companies in the district, which began in 1921. The silver and gold ore were shipped to Douglas for processing. The Stargo mines had been under bond to Phelps Dodge for some time, so finally manager M.J. Hannon decided to sell.[264]

Work along Ryerson Gulch at the start of open-pit operations required the removal of the top layers (over burden) of Clay Mountain to expose the ore body. The operation was a twenty-four-hour, seven-day-a week endeavor, as seven hundred men worked stripping and preparing the ground to expose the huge ore body. This was a tremendous effort by man and machine, blasting and moving tons of rock and dirt. As early as 1928, work began to drain the underground mines around the canyon of water using a 4,300-foot tunnel that was 7½ feet high and 6 feet wide, with smaller branching tunnels connecting to the main line. The tunnel was at the lowest point possible, allowing gravity to do the work.[265] As the pit developed, rail lines were installed at each level to make transporting ore easier. The decision by Phelps Dodge to conduct open-pit operations ensured the demise of Metcalf and Old Morenci but saved Clifton and the company.

The reduction works at the mouth of Morenci Canyon, called Bunkers, was built at a cost of around $6 million. Work on the facility began in the late 1930s, and by 1942, construction was finished and it was processing ore from the new open pit. Approximately twenty-one buildings were erected, including a crushing plant, concentrator, bedding plant, power plant, a huge smelter, a six-hundred-foot smokestack, machine shops, carpenter shop, paint shop, assay office, shower and locker rooms and office buildings. In total, Phelps Dodge spent over $60 million for the entire Morenci mine upgrade and was financially assisted by favorable government loans.[266] A second twin smelter stack, called the converter stack, was completed in early 1969 as part of an $11 million upgrade.[267] The smelter was permanently shut down on December 31, 1984.[268] Both stacks were demolished in 1996.[269]

This smelter had a two-step smelting furnace operation, plus an anode production area where ingots were made. In the first step, crushed ore was sent from the concentrator's bedding plant to the smelter on long conveyor belts, and it was melted in large reverbatory furnaces. Train trolleys carried the reverb's molten waste, called slag, to a massive slag dump around the clock. In the second step, the enriched molten matte was transferred from the reverbs to the converter furnaces by overhead cranes using giant ladles, and the refining was continued. Workers called skimmers regularly collected samples of molten metal from the converters. Convertor slag was collected at the top of the matte, but it still had some copper in it, so it was carefully poured off the top and returned to the reverb furnace. When the converter's matte reached a high percentage of copper (98+ percent), it was sent to the anode area. There, it was poured into molds on a big circular wheel, and the Morenci smelter's finalized product, called ingots or anodes, was formed and cooled, ready for transportation to a final refining smelter in El Paso, Texas.

Company officials and workers gather around James Colquhoun during laying of the cornerstone for the new general office in Clifton. *Courtesy of the Greenlee County Historical Society.*

The business of mining can be complex, and its management is very important. The general office of the Detroit Copper Company in Morenci was built in 1913. It replaced a smaller building that overlooked the smelter. The basement had a darkroom for the company photographer, furnace and coal rooms, closets and storage rooms. The first floor had the general manager's office, an office for the power department superintendent, a room for the telephone exchange and the office for the superintendent of the Morenci Southern Railway. The second floor housed the superintendent of mines, drafting rooms and chief engineer and blueprint rooms. A fireproof vault was on each floor.[270] In the 1960s, a new general office was built at Bunkers near the smelter and is still in use today.

When it was announced that the general office for the Arizona Copper Company would be constructed, it was described as "an ornament to the town."[271] Company president James Colquhoun "wielded the trowel and laid the [corner] stone" at the right front of the building on June 5, 1904.[272] In 1910, an addition on the left half of the building was completed and housed the offices for the Arizona & New Mexico Railway.[273] In later years, this building housed Western Auto Parts, the *Copper Era* and the Valley National Bank. Behind the building was a tunnel leading directly from the Elks Lodge to a cave that held a small casino. It could be entered only by lodge members through a "secret" controlled access door. Profits from the casino went to local charitable causes.[274] Gambling was illegal in Arizona, and the state tried to locate and close down the casino for many years, but the agents were always foiled in their attempts.

The company was at a turning point in the 1930s, as there was a great deal of construction across the district. Chief Engineer Walter C. Lawson and his staff were busy drawing plans and blueprints for all the projects, as mining operations transitioned from underground to open pit. Through his vision and leadership, the company was extremely successful. He retired in 1969 as vice-president and general manager of Phelps Dodge Western Operations. He was inducted into the National Mining Hall of Fame in 1994,[275] and the football stadium at Morenci High School is named in his honor.

Charles E. Mills was the general manager of the Detroit Copper Company from 1897 to 1912. He first worked in Bisbee in 1888 after graduating from the University of Iowa but soon went back to school, attending Harvard University before coming to Morenci. At the outbreak of the Spanish-American War, he left the company to enlist as a private to serve in Teddy Roosevelt's Rough Riders. After the war, he came back to Morenci but left in 1912 for the mines in Miami, Arizona. While in Morenci, he also became a stockholder in the Gila Valley Bank and Trust Company, becoming president in 1908. He merged this bank with the Valley Bank in 1922 to form the Valley National Bank. It became the largest bank in Arizona.[276] Mills' home had a commanding view of Morenci Canyon and the smelter.

Businesses

General stores and mercantiles have been an important part of life in the mining camps. Company employees were able to charge items to their account, and then the money was deducted from their next paycheck. Many employees purchased the company coupon books. Coupons had a cash value but could be used only in the company's stores. Phelps Dodge built stores in Plantsite and Stargo in the 1940s and, in the 1960s, built a large mercantile[277] and shopping center[278] in Plantsite. The grandfather of author Robert A. Chilicky worked at the store in Stargo and later the Plantsite mercantile.

In the 1880s, North Clifton had many saloons, along with the printing office of the *Clifton Clarion*. The publisher moved the paper to Solomonville around 1889, and after several more changes, it survives today as the *Eastern*

Employees of the Arizona Copper Company store in Clifton. This store was across the street from the ice plant. *Gerald D. Hunt personal collection.*

Arizona Courier out of Safford, Arizona. This section of town was primarily residential, but it was also the home of several important businesses. One was the Golden Eagle store, which in 1904 sold dried fish from Alaska for twenty-five cents each.[279]

Clifton's Eastside was the main part of town until businesses and homes were established along Chase Creek and Hill's Addition. Businesses were both large and small. A simple shoeshine stand stood across the street from the Clifton Hotel operated by a man named Long Tom.[280] Fritz Adolphy owned the Mountain Brewery here. It was one of the more popular establishments for thirsty miners to spend their money. Adolphy owned beer halls in St. Louis, Chicago and Salt Lake City, where he adopted over ninety girls throughout the years to serve as waitresses. At that time, women were not allowed to work in a beer hall unless they were the daughter of the owner. He used this loophole to his advantage over the years.[281] In 1886, he built a shooting gallery next to the brewery.[282] Adolphy is buried in the Clifton Cemetery in Ward Canyon.

A narrow suspension bridge across the San Francisco River was just upriver from the current bridge to the Eastside. There were several business advertisements on the bridge, and at one time, a sign above the entrance read, "Sastrería Se Vende Ropa Barata—Mit Simms," indicating that Simms's tailor shop sold inexpensive clothing. Simms later became an Arizona state senator and Arizona secretary of state, and he ran for governor in 1920.[283]

The Library Hall in Clifton was built by the Arizona Copper Company in 1898. Downstairs was a library and post office, and the space was also used to hold company banquets and meetings. Upstairs was a Masonic Hall.[284] In January 1901, the Arizona Copper Company held a lavish dinner here for mine executives and friends. Many toasts were proposed and responded to. Catering was provided by a company from San Francisco, California.[285] The dinner became an annual event. In later years, it became the Clifton branch of the Phelps Dodge Mercantile Company.

One of the most important additions to Morenci was the Detroit Copper Company Store, built in 1901. The stone to build it was quarried one mile below town at the mouth of Morenci Canyon.[286] It replaced a much smaller store, and it rivaled every other store in the region. The interior had high ceilings, polished maple wood floors, silver- and nickel-trimmed display cases and elegant fixtures. Store manager Harry S. Van Gorder helped design the

There were suspension bridges across the San Francisco River in several places at different times. They served foot traffic until bridges that could accommodate automobiles were built. *Robert A. Chilicky personal collection.*

The smallest detail was not overlooked to make each department of the Detroit Copper Company store as organized and fully stocked as possible, while providing outstanding customer service. *Courtesy of the Greenlee County Historical Society.*

layout for the sales floor to optimize floor space and make shopping easier for the customer. The store had four floors and offered a wide range of goods and services. The bottom floor had a service dock to load and unload goods from trains, wagons and trucks. Items were kept in dry or cold storage on this level until needed on the sales floor. A large service elevator was used to move goods to all the floors. The second level, which was the main floor, was men's and women's clothing, footwear, coats and jackets, rugs, hats and shawls, dry and canned goods, jewelry, art and novelty items and a pharmaceutical area that also sold cigars and candy. To the rear of this floor was a tailor department for men and women, hardware, guns, ammunition, photography items, a butcher shop and a cheese department. Taking a grand staircase to the mezzanine and third floor, you would find sewing materials, buttons and cloth, glass, china and porcelain items. Also, burial caskets could be found here. The top floor was devoted to furniture, carpets, rugs, curtains and other home furnishings. Store offices were located on this floor. An internal telephone system connected the departments to one another and with the manager's office. The store even had a reception room for tired shoppers, with racks of magazines and newspapers and stationery if one desired to pen a letter.[287] The store also had the Lamson cash carrier system, a network of electric cables that carried cash payments in metal containers from each department to the central accounting office, then sent the change and receipts back to the department.[288] In later years, a pneumatic tube system was used to transport payments from the sales floor to cashiers. The service lights in and outside the store made for an inspiring scene at night. The sales floor layout went through several changes over the years to bring in new goods and services to meet the evolving needs of the community.

This section of town was called South Clifton in the early days, with the Shannon Copper Company store on the right. *Robert A. Chilicky personal collection.*

In 1901, J.N. McFate constructed a building along Railroad Avenue that became the Young & Clemmons Drugstore.[289] The Shannon Copper Company bought the structure in 1905 to be used for its mercantile and in 1907 built an addition on to the left side of the building. In 1913, the company built a mercantile on Shannon Hill. Its foundation can still be seen today. The Railroad Avenue building was leased to businessmen C.P. Dunn and Felix Brutinel, who in turn leased the bottom floor out to several businesses and converted the upper floor into apartments. As the company was being sold to the Arizona Copper Company, they temporarily acquired use of the building in 1919, then known as the Brutinel Building. All merchandise from the stores on Shannon Hill and Metcalf were moved here to be sold off at greatly reduced prices.[290]

The Chase Creek district was divided into the West Clifton and San Francisco Townsites, with Lynch Street the border between the two. The Spezia & Spezia building was erected in 1913. It has housed several businesses and groups through the years, including the Fraternal Order of Eagles, Aerie Number 1690, the City Hall of Clifton, Co-Operativa Mercantil Mexicana, Freddie Schale's Hardware and now the Greenlee County Historical Society. The Cascarelli building is another important structure, housing at one time the Fernández Mercantile. Originally three stories high, it burned down in 1913. It was rebuilt using bricks from the

An ore train is stopped in front of the Arizona Copper Company store at Coronado. *Courtesy of the Greenlee County Historical Society.*

The new shopping center and theatre in Morenci enhanced the town's retail and entertainment options. *Robert A. Chilicky personal collection.*

original structure.[291] The People's Bank & Trust Company, built in 1918, stands near the entrance of the district. In addition to being a fine financial institution, the bank boasted a ladies-only restroom. No other business in town had one at this time. At the grand opening of the bank, gentlemen were given cigars to enjoy and ladies were presented with carnations.[292] The bank building is now a privately owned boardinghouse. One of the long-standing businesses on the street is Nabor's Corner Barber Shop, owned by Ed and Max Nabor since the 1970s.[293]

The Cash & Carry Market and Roscoe & Company Grocery served Clifton for many years. Gerardo Zorilla built the market, located in South Clifton, in 1929 for his daughter Maria and her husband, Fabian, to run. Their son Lloyd Fernández became the Greenlee County Superior Court judge. This section of town had several Chinese gardens in the early days of Clifton, and the harvests were sold in stands along this section of the road.[294] The Big Dipper restaurant was next door to the Cash & Carry. It was damaged during the 1983 flood and rebuilt as the popular PJ's Café, owned by Jackie Norton.

The contracts to build the Morenci Shopping Center and Royal Theatre were awarded in 1947 at a cost of $320,000.[295] Businesses included the Center Market, Kopper Kettle Kafe, Pine's clothing store, Estes Drug Store, Buffo Jewelry, Joe's Furniture, the post office, Charlie's Five and Dime, Jessie's Beauty Salon, Harrington's Barber Shop, a dry cleaners and a dental office. The Kopper Kettle and Estes Drug were favorite lunch destinations for students. At Estes, they would line up two and three deep at the lunch counter, waiting to eat, listening to the jukebox or looking through the magazine and record racks.

Housing

Just as in other mining towns, the land of Old Morenci and Metcalf was owned by the company. People paid rent on the land, but many of the homes belonged to the residents. In Clifton, Henry Hill began to develop Metz's Flats after purchasing it in 1899.[296] He built a home for himself and his wife, as well as houses for his two daughters, Rosie and Margaret. Other houses nearby were built for company officials. Additional homes and new businesses were erected, and Hill's Addition soon grew into a comfortable residential and retail section of town.

Clifton's Eastside was known as Old Town in the early days. People built their homes up and down the surrounding mountainsides. The Arizona Copper Company residences along the river were the general manager's house and those for store manager E.M. Williams, store purchasing agent J.G. Cooper and chief engineer Spencer Bishop.[297] During World War I, a Victory Garden was planted on the grounds of these residences, growing potatoes and sugar beets.[298] The general manager's house, first occupied by Norman Carmichael, is a magnificent residence. It is by far the largest home in the district, with more than twenty rooms, six bathrooms and a full basement.[299] The company spared no expense in its design and construction to re-invest money into the company and not be taxed by the British government.[300] In 1916, during the strike, an unknown person fired shots at the residence in the middle of the night. It was not known if Carmichael was the target of an assassination plot, and the shooter was never caught.[301]

Shannon Hill had become a vibrant community by the early 1900s. The Shannon Copper Company built a smelter there, and soon families came and called the area home. It was a convenient place to live, being so close to work. Businesses, a school, a store and a church were built to fit the needs of the growing population. In 1906, there was talk of making the Shannon Hill area its own separate town apart from Clifton, to be called Shannon Heights.[302]

With the influx of miners coming to work in the district in the late 1930s as open-pit operations were ramping up, the company quickly realized that

Opposite: Morenci comprises several hills, with houses clinging to all the hillsides. When Old Morenci was torn down, many of the homes were moved to other places. *Robert A. Chilicky personal collection.*

Top: Looking south at North Clifton in the 1890s. The flume for the Arizona Copper Company smelter is running along the base of the mountains at the right. *Courtesy of the Greenlee County Historical Society.*

Bottom: Upper portion of Stargo, 1938. The narrow streets followed the contour of the hillsides. *Robert A. Chilicky personal collection.*

Sunset, Ash and Linden Streets in East Plantsite, 1952. Copper King Mountain rises in the far distance. *Courtesy of the Greenlee County Historical Society.*

more housing was needed. The townsite of Stargo was built in Apache Gulch, with construction starting in 1937. The first homes had copper roofs.[303] Later, when more houses were built, all the homes had asphalt roof shingles. Garages were built in a group for nearby houses, while some homes had their own garage. Stairways up the hills connected the home street level to the garage. Tales of witches in Stargo and Morenci were told throughout the years, with some residents reporting seeing fireballs rolling up the surrounding hills.[304]

The Stargo Garden Club was formed in 1939[305] to make the new housing area of Stargo more pleasant to live in. People were encouraged to plant trees and gardens. Annual prizes were awarded to the best yards. Children were also encouraged to participate, winning prizes in their own category. Many of the trees and bushes were retrieved from the yards of Metcalf, which was being abandoned. Planting soil was brought in by burros from Eagle Creek.[306] Soil was also brought in by pickup trucks from the San Francisco River.

The area known as Plantsite was created in the 1940s, and soon the construction of housing there began in what was known as Sites 1, 2 and 3. Ten homes were built for mine management near the new reduction works on what would become Buena Vista Street in 1940, and four homes were constructed on what was known as West Stargo for mine executives.[307] This area became known as Cedar Loop. More houses would be built at East Plantsite and the lower section called The Flats.

One aspect of housing in Morenci is the fact that segregation was implemented. Stargo was designated for White families. Site 3 and Gila

Street in East Plantsite housed Hispanics and several Black families. Tent City near Bunkers was for the Indian population. As years went by, the "old way" of thinking faded, and this practice ended.

Transportation and Railroads

Travel between the towns of the county was an early issue. From 1899 to 1919, a toll road existed between Solomonville and Coronado Station on the Gila River. The tollhouse was known as *La Garita*. The toll was fifty cents per team and ten cents for each horse and rider. In time, the toll was reduced to thirty cents per team. After a few years, lunch was provided for a small fee for travelers wanting a meal. Before the toll road through the Black Hills was built, the road between Clifton and Solomonville went through the Ash Springs / Duncan area, and the trip usually took three days. Author Gerald D. Hunt's grandmother recalled trips from Franklin to Safford to visit family that took two days by wagon. A young freighter, Francisco Montes, and friends Victoriano Carrasco, Andrés Serna and Emilio Lopera would occasionally take a shortcut through the Black Hills. They decided to capitalize on this and built the toll road using simple hand tools. Material for the tollhouse came from the Solomonville / San José area.[308] In 1901, they sold their interests in the road to Luther Greene.[309] Originally the road went to Sheldon to connect with the Arizona & New Mexico Railway, but when Greene took over, he rerouted it to Coronado Station on the south side of

Children enjoy the view from the Clifton-Duncan Highway, with the Arizona Copper Company smelter in operation down on the right. Much of this road is still visible today. *Courtesy of the Greenlee County Historical Society.*

the Gila River just southeast of Guthrie. Also, the mining companies at Ash Peak built ore bins at Coronado Station in 1906 so they could ship their ore by rail to the Shannon Copper Company smelter in Clifton.[310] The tollhouse and much of the road wcrc in Graham County, but it was an important part of the early development of Greenlee County.

Travel in and out of Clifton in the early days took travelers over a steep and winding road high above the Arizona Copper Company (later Phelps Dodge) smelter at Smelter Hill. At the top of the mountain, known today as Table Top, travelers could turn right to continue to Safford or turn left to proceed to Duncan. The road passed through the area of the current hamlets of Verde Lee and Loma Linda. The scenic old dirt road to Safford is now called the Black Hills Back Country By-Way. In September 1920, the road up Ward Canyon from town—up to this point was a wagon path to the cemetery—was widened and improved,[311] replacing the road near the smelter.

Local businessman Delbert Potter was instrumental in promoting better roads for the district and in bringing Clifton into the national spotlight. He was vice-president of the Arizona chapter of the Ocean-to-Ocean Highway Association.[312] He labored for years to have the intercontinental highway pass through Phoenix, Globe, Safford, Clifton and on to Silver City, New Mexico, via Mule Creek. He would travel the state and country to speak to investors and invite touring groups who were traveling the country along the proposed route to come to Clifton to promote the endeavor.

As means of transportation became modernized, the dangerous road leading north of Metcalf along Chase Creek needed to be improved. The section of highway north of the Metcalf area is known as the Switchbacks. To gain elevation, the road hugged the contours of the mountainside. The original road up the mountain was steep and narrow. An early pioneer named Charles A. Hamblin was killed along the old road in 1899 near the top. He and his brother ran a freight business. While the brothers were going down the mountain, the wagon slipped off the road. Charles's brother, though severely injured, managed to make his way to Metcalf for help.[313] Hamblin's grave can be seen high above one of the curves along the road.

The tunnel work in Morenci Canyon on the Clifton-Morenci Highway was completed in July 1949, and a few weeks later the tunnel road was finalized. It was built to eliminate the narrow, curving road on the north side of the canyon that wrapped around the mountain. Although the old road offered spectacular views, it was dangerous, especially at the blind curve around the mountain cliff. The 410-foot tunnel was the longest in the state

Top: The famous Switchbacks near Morenci along the Coronado Trail. *Courtesy of the Greenlee County Historical Society.*

Bottom: Needle's Eye on the Mule Creek Road. *Courtesy of the Greenlee County Historical Society.*

highway system[314] until the 1,200-foot Queen Creek Tunnel was completed in 1952 just east of Superior on Highway 60. There is a local tradition of honking your vehicle horn when you travel through the Morenci tunnel.

On the Clifton–Silver City (New Mexico) Road stood Needle's Eye, a huge rock formation that the road tunneled through. The road, completed in 1922, made the trip safer and faster between the two towns. Owen O'Dell and William C. Packer of Duncan helped build the road, using TNT on the last three miles, which had numerous switchbacks and steep cliffs.[315] In a nearby canyon is the cave hideout of an outlaw gang called the "High Fives" led by William "Black Jack" Christian. In April 1897, law enforcement officials from Clifton located the hideout. Following a gun battle, Black Jack lay dead. His body was taken to Clifton for positive identification.[316] Today, the canyon, cave and a nearby campground bear his name.

Chase Creek Canyon provided spectacular views and was known throughout the region for its unique beauty. Connecting Metcalf and Clifton required excellent engineering for the road and two rail lines. Retaining walls along the canyon helped with road, vehicle and railroad safety. The Lesinsky brothers built the Coronado line in 1879,[317] and it was one of the first railroads in Arizona. The Shannon line was built in 1909–10 by Morenci Southern contractor J.S. Antonelle and Clifton contractors O.J. Cotey and L.B. Elliott, along with other subcontractors.[318] Construction of the Shannon line did not affect trains of the Coronado line, even with all the blasting and earth excavation nearby. After the railroads were abandoned, the highway passed through several of the old railroad tunnels, and black stains from the locomotive's smoke were visible. A cut in the mountain where the Shannon line went through is visible near Sacred Heart Cemetery.

On May 10, 1900, a trestle on the Arizona & New Mexico Railway just south of Clifton collapsed as a train was headed to Guthrie. Charlie Shannon

A train of the Morenci Southern Railway navigates Loop Number 5 in Morenci. *Courtesy of the Greenlee County Historical Society.*

of the Shannon Copper Company was in the passenger car but was unhurt because the back half of the train stayed on the track. Thomas Simpson, who would later own the Simpson Hotel in Duncan, was the engineer on the train during the accident.[319]

After Phelps Dodge acquired the properties and assets of the Detroit Copper Company in 1897, they realized a railroad was needed to transport material in and out of Morenci. The Morenci Southern Railway was the answer. It operated between 1901 and 1922. After a few years, passenger cars were purchased, and people could enjoy a thrilling trip along the "Corkscrew Route of America" between Guthrie and Morenci. Due to the elevation changes, the line overlapped itself via loops. The first loop was near the crossing of the San Francisco River, and it used the surrounding terrain and a tunnel to gain elevation. The other four loops, using wooden trestles, were in Morenci Canyon. Repairs of the aging trestles eventually became too costly. Starting in 1913, with the removal of Loop 4, the company installed switchbacks.[320] This allowed for safer travel, but the trip took longer. Many remnants of the line are still visible along the route.

The small narrow-gauge engines of the Coronado Railroad served the district for many years. Engine Number 8, built in 1897 and retired in 1922, has been on display in Clifton since 1937.[321] Tommy Sidebotham and others were instrumental in restoring the engine and finding a place to display it. The engine mainly worked between Clifton and the Longfellow Incline but occasionally transported ore cars up to Metcalf. For many years, the engine was on display in front of the Phelps Dodge Mercantile but is now next to the Cliff Jail.

Floods

The floods that have hit the county over the years have been very destructive. The flood of December 1906 was one of the more devastating ones in Clifton. This flood was made worse than others when the tailings dam broke in Ryerson Gulch near Morenci, causing a fifteen-foot wall of mine waste and water to rush down Chase Creek. The total collapse of the dam took twenty minutes, giving mine officials time to send a telegraph to Clifton warning of the impending disaster. Several lives were lost, and there was great damage to homes and businesses. The people of Chase Creek sued the Detroit Copper Company. After several years of court proceedings, they won a judgment to help rebuild. The Eastside was also hit very hard.

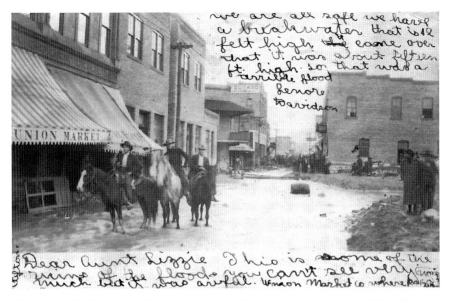

The sender of this card is telling family of the wall of water that came down Chase Creek during the 1906 flood. *Courtesy of the Greenlee County Historical Society.*

Many structures were adobe, which melted away in the raging water. Most of this side of town was under about four feet of water. The high ground of Shannon Hill became a safe place for people to seek refuge. The flood knocked out water and electric service, so the hills around Clifton were lit up with campfires as people took to higher ground.[322]

There have been numerous attempts to help control floodwaters. In 1910, the Arizona Copper Company poured slag on either side of Chase Creek through Clifton to build up a barrier.[323] Slag walls have also been built along the San Francisco River. Later, rocks from a nearby quarry were used to build walls. These walls had a secondary effect as cattle were driven down the creek and river from the ranches north of Metcalf and Clifton. The barriers helped keep cattle herds out of the town when they were being driven to stockyards. Today, Chase Creek is completely closed off about a mile above Clifton.

The flood through Clifton on January 19, 1916, was also disastrous. Telegraphs from forest rangers in the northern part of the county warned residents of the heavy rains. News was also flashed on the screens at the moving-picture theaters in town. Although very destructive, the flood could have been far worse, but a sudden drop in temperature turned rain into snow in the mountains. During this flood, a footbridge across the river in North Clifton was demolished.[324]

The flood of 1916 was an example of the fury the San Francisco River can unleash. Note the huge wave. *Courtesy of the Greenlee County Historical Society.*

The floods of 1972 and 1983 have been well-documented, but the magnitude and damaging effects they had on the county, especially on Clifton and Duncan, are worth mention and remembrance here. Homes were destroyed, and businesses wiped out, many never to return. As a result, numerous families decided to move elsewhere.

STRIKES

Disputes between workers and company management have been a common occurrence in the district. The 1903 labor strike was one of these episodes and was one of the most violent conflicts in the history of the district. More than eight hundred soldiers from Fort Grant, Fort Huachuca and the Arizona National Guard were sent to Morenci and bivouacked next to the Morenci Club and Detroit Copper Company store and on the surrounding hills. They, along with local law enforcement, monitored strike activities. Also, the Arizona Rangers were summoned to Morenci to help keep the peace. Martial law was declared in Morenci, and anyone caught outside after curfew was subject to arrest. Soldiers patrolled Clifton, Morenci and Metcalf and often confronted armed strikers. County sheriff James Parks deputized about twenty men in Clifton and came to Morenci. He and his men and some of the Rangers stopped seven hundred armed strikers led by a man called "Three-Finger" Jack Laustaunau. They were intent on doing damage to the concentrator at Ryerson Gulch. The sheriff had nerves of steel and a reputation for not backing down from a fight. Jack and his men surrounded the officers, but the sheriff drew his gun, aimed at Jack and did not take his eye or gun off him. After some tense minutes, and not seeing anything good in his favor, Jack and the strikers backed down.[325] The Shannon, Detroit and Arizona Copper Companies presented Parks with a Tiffany gold watch. Ninety-four diamonds were set into the initials engraved on the cover.[326] If the strike was not enough, a sudden cloudburst in Chase Creek Canyon just south of Metcalf caused a flood to hit Clifton on June 9, causing thousands of dollars in damage and the loss of twenty to thirty lives. Businessman John Gatti happened to be in the area and saw the water racing down the canyon. He turned his horse toward Clifton at full speed and waved and yelled. He managed to warn and save some people, but the torrent of water was too fast.[327]

The strike of 1915 was another violent period in the history of the district. The Western Federation of Miners, headquartered in Denver, Colorado, sent representatives to the district to organize the strikers. Workers were often dragged from their homes in the middle of the night, beaten and held at gunpoint to pledge allegiance to the unions. The railroads were not immune to violence. The managers of the Detroit, Shannon and Arizona Copper Companies were taken to Lordsburg, New Mexico, for their safety. Strikers found out about this, and when the Arizona & New Mexico train arrived back at the Clifton station, the engineer, Thomas Simpson, and his

Soldier's camp in Morenci during the 1903 strike. *Courtesy of the Greenlee County Historical Society.*

Shown here is a rally during the 1915 strike near the Arizona Copper Company Drug Department and Library Hall in Clifton. *Courtesy of the Greenlee County Historical Society.*

fireman, Walter Penn, were beaten with clubs. Later that night, a mob went to their homes to continue the assault, but both men escaped to Duncan in automobiles.[328] Duncan became a haven for workers and their families to get away from the violence. A camp was set up near town for families and single men to call home. Businesses in town provided necessities, and the copper companies paid all costs.[329]

The strike of the early 1980s was the last to be held. In many cases, families were on both sides of the dispute, and the sentiment spilled into the schools. Students transferred in both directions between Clifton and Morenci schools at the insistence of parents so they would not be associated with kids of families from the other side. In August 1983, toward the end of a ten-day "cooling off" period, over one thousand Arizona National Guard troops and Arizona Department of Public Safety (DPS) officers were ordered to the district to help keep the peace. It was the largest deployment of military and police in the history of the state.[330]

HOSPITALS

Mine accidents required immediate aid, and a medical facility was needed for the townsfolk. The first recorded hospital in the district was next to Casa Grande on Clifton's Eastside.[331] The Arizona Copper Company built its hospital in Clifton in 1900, and a second building was added in 1903.[332] In 1907, Tom Sidebotham, a foreman at the Detroit Copper Company concentrator at Longfellow, was involved in an accident on the Longfellow Incline. He broke his leg and recovered at this hospital.[333] In the late 1980s, after the hospital was torn down, Sidebotham Park was built where the hospital once stood. The park was named for Tommy Sidebotham, Tom's nephew, who was a popular law enforcement officer in Clifton for many years. The Arizona Copper Company also had hospitals in Metcalf and Morenci. The Detroit Copper Company built a new hospital in the Fairplay area of Morenci in 1902.[334] The Shannon Copper Company had its hospital in Clifton in the general location of today's Go-Go Gas. It was in service until 1919.[335]

In early 1940, a hospital was constructed in Morenci for $150,000. It was X-shaped, with a surgery wing and a wing with two three-bed and three four-bed wards. A third wing had eight private rooms and two semi-private rooms. The fourth wing had a reception room, doctor's offices,

Arizona Copper Company hospital, Clifton. *Courtesy of the Greenlee County Historical Society.*

Morenci Hospital. This facility has a twin in Douglas, Arizona, built at the same time. *Courtesy of the Greenlee County Historical Society.*

nurse stations and the administration office.[336] The Morenci Women's Club raised money to purchase an iron lung to help treat patients with polio and respiratory problems.[337] In 1969, the hospital was donated to the detention facility at Fort Grant, Arizona. Boys from the facility tore it down and rebuilt it at that location.[338]

Finally, a modern hospital opened in Plantsite on February 19, 1968, at a cost of $1.8 million. It was of Spanish design to go with the motif of the new shopping center. The hospital was designed by the architecture firm Lescher & Mahoney, with Mardian Construction Company the builders. It had the latest medical essentials, along with kitchen and laundry services. The nursery included rocking chairs to give new mothers a feel as if they were at their own home taking care of their baby. In the middle of the building was a patio with a fountain displaying multicolored lights.[339]

MILITARY

The county has a proud history of military service among its citizens. As a result of the 1903 strike, a cavalry unit was formed in Morenci to help protect citizens and businesses.[340] The Second Cavalry Troop of the First Arizona Infantry Regiment was placed under the command of Captain Alexander Tuthill. He went on to lead the First Arizona Infantry Regiment

The soldiers of the Clifton unit trained hard and played hard. Here they enjoy a jug of whiskey from the Old Lewis Hunter Distillery, compliments of businessman Peter Riley. *Courtesy of the Greenlee County Historical Society.*

A large crowd gathered to see the boys off to training, May 1918. *Gerald D. Hunt personal collection.*

during the campaign against Pancho Villa in 1916–17. H.S. Van Gorder, the manager of the Detroit Copper Company store and the cashier at the Gila Valley Bank and Trust, served as a second lieutenant in the troop.[341] Before he entered military service, Tuthill was the chief surgeon for the Detroit Copper Company,[342] and after his military service he became president of the state medical society and state superintendent of public health.[343]

Company F, First Battalion, Eleventh Infantry of the National Guard of Arizona was mustered into service in 1908 and was commanded by Captain Paul Reisinger.[344] The unit was a source of pride for the people of Clifton, as the soldiers were often seen marching on the parade field in South Clifton or honing their marksmanship skills on the rifle range. Along with the other Arizona National Guard units, including the cavalry unit from Morenci, the Clifton soldiers traveled to Phoenix, Prescott or Douglas for camp every summer. There they competed in company drill, marksmanship and other military skills activities.

Young men were quick to answer the call of freedom as the United States was preparing to enter World War I. On May 25, 1918, forty-six men from towns around the county and twenty-nine from towns from all over the region gathered in Clifton and were put under the command of Captain Rodney Ellis. Dances were held at the high school auditorium and at the Princess Theater. On the morning of May 27, with Clifton mayor O.J. Cotey leading and two brass bands providing music, they marched from the courthouse to the Reardon Hotel. They boarded a train of the Arizona & New Mexico Railway and headed to Camp Cody, New Mexico, near Deming to begin their training. Local ladies prepared bags for each soldier that included items they may need while away from home.[345] Captain William Wallace Colquhoun, son of former Arizona Copper Company president James Colquhoun, was killed in action during the Battle of Loos in northeastern France on September 25, 1915. He was in the Eleventh Highland Light Infantry in the British army and died leading his men in battle.[346] He had attended Clifton schools as a boy.

3

THE WHITE MOUNTAINS

Rugged Paradise

Whe most people think of Arizona, the vision of an unforgiving desert comes to mind. Just north of Morenci, however, the elevation is about five thousand feet and quickly rises to over eight thousand feet as you head toward Hannagan Meadow. The numerous lakes, rivers and streams have kept anglers happy for generations. The first fish hatchery in Arizona was built in September 1923 and operational by April 1924, making it more

Beaver Head Lodge, just north of Hannagan Meadow, welcomed generations of adventurers and travelers exploring the White Mountains. *Courtesy of the Arizona Historical Society Library & Archives, Oliver Ambrose Risdon Photograph Collection, PC 204_F.12_A.*

convenient to stock the rivers and lakes. It was located about ten miles south of Springerville along the south fork of the Little Colorado River.[347] It also ensured that fishermen in Arizona did not have to leave the state to find good fishing. Before the stocking programs, many anglers traveled out of state every year to enjoy their sport, resulting in a loss of revenue for the state. Many activities in the mountains were planned out months in advance. In 1946, for example, big-game hunters could contact Jes L. Burke at the Beaver Head Lodge to go on bear- and lion-hunting trips, with Burke providing the hounds and horses. Others could enjoy the Sprucedale Ranch, operated by Walter L. Wiltbank and family. The ranch offered to teach people how to break and ride horses and brand calves, and it organized fishing and hunting trips using pack horses to transport the gear.[348]

THE CORONADO TRAIL

A narrow, twisting road best suited for wagons had already existed from Metcalf to Grey's Peak in the early 1900s. Expanding that section and continuing the road north over steep slopes and high mountains and skirting deep canyons took expert planning, engineering and hard work by the crews who blasted their way through the mountains. In 1922, Clifton firm Cotey & Black was awarded the contract[349] to build the section of road roughly between 4 Bar Mesa and Alpine. Near the completion of the Coronado Trail in 1926, Cotey won a bid to lay down gravel on the road in the Rose Peak area.[350] The road was mostly completed by the forest service and county road crews. Until the 1960s, most of it was unpaved. The road was brutal on vehicles. The highway department installed water tanks every few miles to ensure that travelers had enough water for their radiators to help prevent engines from overheating.

One of the popular destinations along the road is Hannagan Meadow. The naming of the location is one of legend. The story goes that in the late 1800s a man named Robert Hannagan found his way to this area. He was a miner and saloonkeeper but became involved in cattle ranching after settling in New Mexico and Arizona. As time went on, he became in debt to brothers from another ranch for $1,200, which he avoided paying. One day, the brothers found out which stage he was on and pulled him from the coach and chained him to a tree. Word was sent to his son in New Mexico to pay the debt or Hannagan would not be released. His son quickly paid the debt, and Hannagan was set free. The naming of the meadow was decided by a

Contractor Robert S. Black and his wife, Soledad, in camp while the Coronado Trail was under construction, 1922. Robert S. Black Jr. is playing behind the wheel of the car. *Courtesy of Robert S. Black III.*

coin flip between Hannagan and a rancher named Toles Cosper. Over time, others in the area wanted to name it after Cosper, but he was a man of his word and would not agree.[351]

A grand two-day celebration was held at Hannagan Meadow in June 1926 as people came from all over the region to celebrate the road's completion. There were many events, including a rodeo, Indian music and ceremonies, with a wide range of food, including small game, trout caught at the nearby streams and lakes and bear meat. Many of the Indian tribes of Arizona and New Mexico were represented, including the White Mountain Apaches, led by their great leader, Alchesay. The Indians provided the main entertainment by performing several dances. The main dance was the Devil Dance, which started at sundown and went nonstop until sunrise, complete with the steady beating of drums and the glow of bonfires reflecting off the painted bodies of 125 performers. A huge platform was constructed for the event from which dignitaries gave speeches and a jazz orchestra provided dance music. Mayor Peter Riley of Clifton was the chairman of the event, and Governor George W.P. Hunt

Arizona governor George W.P. Hunt is with a group of White Mountain Apaches during the dedication celebration of the Coronado Trail. *Arizona State Library, Archives and Public Records, Archives and Records Management Branch MG 25 George W.P. Hunt.*

was the keynote speaker, dressed in his trademark white suit. He unveiled the plaque dedicating the road. It was made of copper from the Morenci mine.[352] DeWitt Cosper, the son of Toles, received a permit to operate a store during the Coronado Trail dedication celebration. It is not clear who built the original lodge at the meadow, but a few cabins were available during the celebration.[353]

Another famous location along the Coronado Trail, just south of Blue Vista on the Mogollon Rim, was the Arrow Tree near mile marker 223. Over the years, archers had taken aim with their bows to add to the collection of arrows embedded into the tree. Many arrows hit their mark, but countless missed the tree and rained down into the canyon. No one knows who first took aim at the tree and started this landmark, but generations of hunters and tourists were grateful for this often-mentioned location. Sadly, it did not survive a storm in January 2019, and the tree came crashing down, with the top section falling on the highway.

EDUCATION

The one-room schoolhouse on the Blue River. *Courtesy of the Greenlee County Historical Society.*

The county enjoyed many school districts throughout the years. The larger schools were too far away for the children of the many ranches that operated in the mountains, so often a simple schoolhouse was constructed. District Number 22 along the Blue River was one of these districts. By law, a minimum of eight school-aged children was required to form a district. Sometimes, the rural areas had a hard time with this requirement, such as Benton School District Number 23. Its attendance fell below that number and in 1909 was discontinued and absorbed by the Blue District.[354] The Eagle Creek School became School District Number 45. The district encompassed a large area that included much of the northwest part of the county. In 1914, the school operated on a budget of $850 and over the years has served as the polling place for elections. By comparison, Clifton schools had a budget of $40,355 that same year.[355]

ENTERTAINMENT

Living in the mountains was not an easy way of life, yet ranching has a long and important history in Arizona and Greenlee County. The Double Circle Ranch in the Eagle Creek area was unquestionably the largest ranch in the mountains, but other ranches flourished as well. The XXX Ranch, owned by Fred Fritz along the Blue River, was one of them. Some of the other ranches in the area were the Four Drag, 6K6, AD Bar, 7+A, T Link, Tule Springs and Deerhead.[356] Being so remote required a family to live off the land, and sometimes they would go for months without seeing others from outside the area. Work in sawmills and on ranches was tough. Having an item that some would consider a luxury could make life more enjoyable. A possession such as a piano can bring the joy of music and song into the home and make life on the ranch a little more civilized. This was the case for the Wilson family living near

Eagle Creek in 1915. The daughter of rancher T.P. Wilson missed her beloved piano, which they had to leave behind when they moved to the mountains. Wilson wanted to make her happy, so he had the piano they had left back in Kansas shipped by rail all the way to Metcalf. Since he did not have the means to transport the piano to his ranch, he enlisted the help of thirty-five men who were looking for work, since they were on strike from the mines. He paid them $225, and the men were eager to help. They wrapped the piano with blankets and cord and then attached two pipes so that rotating teams could carry it. Wilson headed home, eager for the crew's arrival at the ranch. Around noon the next day, a crew member appeared carrying the chair. Shortly after that, the rest of the group came into view with the piano. Friends and family had gathered, and a loud cheer erupted for the safe arrival of the men and the treasured cargo. Not one scratch was on the piano, and Wilson threw a party that night to honor the men who had carried it. The daughter played during the celebration and entertained locals for many years after.[357]

Mining and Forest Management

Early miners were lured to the district by reports of gold along the Eagle River (Creek) Canyon. For a short time, two mills were on the river near Gold Gulch operated by the Home Copper Company.[358] The Arizona Copper Company operated an aerial tram from the top of Coronado Mountain to the river. The Coronado Trail also helped open the mountains for development through logging and lumber mills, such as the facility at Stray Horse at the bottom of Five Mile Hill.

In 1926, a ranger station was built near Eagle River (Creek), which was in the Crook National Forest. Two houses from Metcalf were dismantled and brought in to build the station.[359] The Honeymoon District had a station starting in 1907.[360] It was first called Reno Ranger Station, but the name was changed to Honeymoon when Forest Ranger John Wheatley took his bride there soon after their wedding.[361]

The Hannagan Meadow Ranger Station was built in 1912 and was the first structure built at the meadow. The station supported fire lookouts and firefighters, and the surrounding meadows had long been used for livestock grazing. In 1939, employees of the Apache National Forest petitioned to save the station for historical purposes. Sadly, the forest service destroyed it by fire in 1956 as a new facility was being completed.[362]

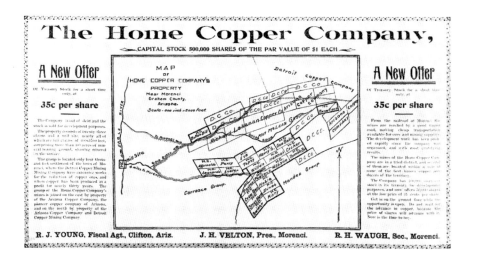

Top: Advertisement for the Home Copper Company from the January 9, 1912 *Copper Era*. *Courtesy of newspapers.com.*

Bottom: Ranger station at Eagle River (Creek). *Courtesy of the Greenlee County Historical Society.*

Opposite: Hannagan Meadow Ranger Station. *Robert A. Chilicky personal collection.*

Ranger Station, Hannigan's Meadows, White Mountains, Arizona

INDIAN TROUBLE

As noted, residents of the county had a long struggle with Indians, and the ranchers in the mountains were no exception. Soon after Geronimo broke away from the San Carlos Reservation, many ranchers and their families living along the San Francisco and Blue Rivers sought refuge in Clifton. They established a camp four miles above Clifton at a place called De Parti's Flat, named for a local Italian family. Several other families and individuals were camped there, including Mason Greenlee and William Sparks, who was a skilled trapper, peace officer and author of *The Apache Kid* and other stories. One man in camp, Jim Rasberry, who had a cabin on the Blue, got impatient and headed back up the river, not listening to the warnings of the others. A few days went by without a word from Jim, so a posse was formed to check on him. Their worst fears were realized; Jim was found dead in his cabin with several arrows in him. Other people did not escape to the safety of Clifton, including William Benton, who was killed while plowing his field. Some were able to fight off the Indians who attacked their cabins. Frank Manning was alerted by his dog Dandy and was able to barricade his door as the Indians tried to get inside. Manning eventually made it to Clifton but kept on going to Mexico and never returned.[363]

Civilian Conservation Corps

During the Great Depression, the county used the services of the Civilian Conservation Corps (CCC). In 1933, President Franklin D. Roosevelt signed the Emergency Conservation Work (EWC) Act that created the program. Regular army officers were assigned to the camps; Arizona was under the Eighth Corps.[364] The camps provided young men the opportunity for work while taking advantage of the education programs, religious services, health and medical services and even athletics. The CCC began building worker camps across the nation and state, including several in Greenlee County. The Slick Rock Camp was located approximately twenty-one miles southwest of Duncan. Another was located one mile north of Duncan. A camp was built on the C.A. Ranch near present-day Three Way. In the White Mountains, camps were near Honeymoon, Juan Miller north of Granville, the Blue River and on the East Fork of the Black River at Buffalo Crossing.[365] Near the Buffalo Crossing camp was one of the largest beaver dams in the state.[366] At first, the CCC workers lived in tents as they began construction on more permanent buildings for storage, sleeping quarters, recreation and mess halls. The Buffalo Crossing boys built a four-seat outhouse on the hillside behind the bunkhouse that had a cement floor, magazine racks and a large picture window looking out over the stream and meadow below.

Playing sports was a favorite activity in the camps. The boys worked hard, and organized sporting events were welcomed. The CCC baseball team at Buffalo Crossing was called the Blue Buffalos. There were players from both the Blue River and Buffalo Crossing camps, so the team combined their names and created their distinct logo.[367] The different camps also had football teams. In 1935, football was reinstated as a team sport at Clifton High School, and they played against teams from the Duncan and U-Diamond camps.[368]

Even today, the work that these young men did is evident. They performed erosion control and built water conservation dams, fire lookout towers, fire roads, recreational facilities, fences, cattle guards, bridges and culverts. Additionally, the men planted trees, restored habitat and stocked streams with fish. They gained experience in over one hundred different types of work. Education was a big part of the program, and many received their high school diplomas while serving in the program. In October 1940, Greenlee County Schools superintendent Douglas Brubaker spoke at graduation ceremonies at the Buffalo Crossing camp.[369] When mining started up again at the end of the 1930s, many camp participants found work in the mines

Entrance to the Buffalo Crossing camp. *Courtesy of Robert Moore.*

Boys of the Blue Buffalos baseball team. *Courtesy of Robert Moore.*

and brought excellent experience to help them find employment. Many men returned from their work in the camps to live in Greenlee's towns and raised families. It was a winning program, from benefiting the environment and agriculture to providing unemployed young men with an education and employable skills.

The impact of the beauty, resources and industry of the White Mountains on the history of the county is immeasurable. Residents of Arizona have long known of the natural and man-made resources of the mountains. The sound of a stream flowing through a mountain meadow and cool, pine-scented breezes whispering through the forest make a trip to the high country very pleasant. The families who have lived here have enjoyed the crisp, high elevations and endured harsh winter conditions and isolation. If you could ask them, they wouldn't have it any other way. They epitomized the unwavering spirit of Greenlee County.

NOTES

Introduction

1. "Coronado Trail from Clifton to Springerville Opens White Mountain paradise," *Arizona Republican* (Phoenix, AZ), May 26, 1926, 14.
2. "Historical Sketch of Greenlee County," *Copper Era* (Clifton, AZ), May 20, 1933, Arizona Historical Society Library & Archives, Tucson, Arizona, 1.
3. Myrick, *Railroads of Arizona*, 124.
4. Cole, *Century Has Passed*, 153.
5. "Apache County," *Arizona Citizen* (Tucson, AZ), February 28, 1879, 1.
6. "Apache Affairs," *Arizona Star* (Tucson, AZ), June 19, 1879, 1.
7. "Graham County," *Arizona Weekly Citizen* (Tucson, AZ), May 1, 1881, 2.
8. "Against Division," *Clifton (AZ) Clarion*, January 28, 1885, 3.
9. "Ruffianly Assault," *Clifton Clarion*, February 25, 1885, 3.
10. "Proposed New County," *Copper Era*, January 10, 1901, 2.
11. Patton, "History of Clifton," 225–28.
12. "The Passing of a Pioneer," *Copper Era*, April 16, 1903, 2.
13. "Mining Notes," *Copper Era*, March 11, 1909, 2.
14. "Duncan Is Ambitious," *Copper Era*, November 29, 1906, 2.
15. "Clifton County Seat Club," *Copper Era*, February 24, 1910, 2.
16. "Election Returns," *Copper Era*, November 11, 1910, 2.
17. "New County of Greenlee Makes Its Official Bow," *Copper Era*, January 6, 1911, 1.

18. "New Courthouse Is Occupied by Officials," *Copper Era*, September 6, 1912, 1.

19. Cole, *Century Has Passed*, 258.

20. "Copper Era Under Water." *Copper Era*, October 3, 1983, Greenlee County Historical Society, Clifton, Arizona, 2.

21. "Hank's Way: Supervisor Wants to Move Greenlee County Seat," *Arizona Republic* (Phoenix, AZ), June 11, 1984, section B, 1.

22. "Copper Ore Put Clifton on the Map," *Arizona Republic*, October 4, 1998, section T, 1.

23. "Town Celebrates Admission as New State," *Copper Era*, February 16, 1912, 1.

24. "Lincoln's Birthday to Witness State Admission," *Copper Era*, February 9, 1912, 1.

25. "Park Program Is Approved," *Arizona Republic*, February 16, 1936, section 4, 1.

26. "Coronado Pageants Honor Anniversary," *Arizona Republic*, November 17, 1940, section 2, 10.

27. "Clifton Entrada Cast Is Selected," *Arizona Republic*, August 16, 1940, section 1, 10.

28. Clark, interview with Filmore and Yiada Stanton.

29. "Clifton Gives Conquistador Play Tonight," *Arizona Republic*, August 31, 1940, section 1, 1.

30. "Clifton Selects Coronado Cast," *Arizona Republic*, August 28, 1940, section 1, 4.

31. "Spun-Copper Bowl Believed Relic of Coronado's Trek," *Arizona Republic*, August 21, 1940, section 1, 5.

32. "Clifton Entrada Is Big Success," *Arizona Republic*, September 4, 1940, section 2, 1.

33. "Coronado Trail for Road Name Proves Popular," *Arizona Republican*, May 16, 1926, section 6, 7.

Chapter 1

34. Burgess, *Mt. Graham Profiles*, 116.

35. Cole, *Century Has Passed*, 9.

36. "Life and Career of Ralston," *Arizona Weekly Miner* (Prescott, AZ), September 10, 1875, 2.

37. Lunt.

38. "Territorial News," *Arizona Citizen*, May 12, 1883, 1.
39. "Captain Gordon's Command," *Arizona Daily Star* (Tucson, AZ), June 14, 1882, 4.
40. Cole, *Century Has Passed*, 133.
41. "Franklin," *Graham Guardian* (Safford, AZ), November 13, 1896, 1.
42. Cole, *Century Has Passed*, 96.
43. "Arizona Copper Co.," *Tucson (AZ) Citizen*, January 7, 1883, 3.
44. Myrick, *Railroads of Arizona*, 62.
45. Ibid., 65–66.
46. "Arizona News," *Arizona Weekly Citizen*, July 28, 1883, 1.
47. "Arizona News," *Arizona Weekly Citizen*, August 18, 1883, 4.
48. Myrick, *Railroads of Arizona*, 65.
49. "The Arizona and New Mexico Railway Company," *Arizona Republican*, June 17, 1906, 12.
50. "Official Statement of Killed and Wounded," *Arizona Weekly Miner*, May 19, 1882, 2.
51. "Governor's Proclamation," *Clifton Clarion*, June 3, 1885, 3.
52. "Capt. Ford's Report," *Clifton Clarion*, June 10, 1885, 2.
53. "That Papoose," *Weekly Arizona Miner*, June 12, 1885, 1.
54. Burgess, *Mt. Graham Profiles*, 144–46.
55. "Arizona Rangers," *Arizona Daily Star*, August 10, 1885, 4.
56. Cole, *Century Has Passed*, 140–41.
57. Ibid., 140–42.
58. "New Methodist Church," *Duncan (AZ) Arizonian*, April 9, 1913, 1.
59. Cole, *Century Has Passed*, 100.
60. "Duncan Donations," *Arizona Republic*, March 24, 1951, 3.
61. Cole, *Century Has Passed*, 101.
62. *Duncan Valley News*, 6.
63. Cole, *Century Has Passed*, 100.
64. "$300,000 Fire in Small Town of Duncan Leaves Big Scars," *Arizona Daily Star*, July 19, 1992, section B, 1.
65. Cole, *Century Has Passed*, 71.
66. "P.D. Mercantile Co. Encourages Trade at Home," *Copper Era*, July 14, 1922, 2.
67. Lunt.
68. "Picture Shows for Farmers," *Copper Era*, August 25, 1922, 2.
69. "Greenlee Ministers Meet," *Arizona Republic*, May 16, 1942, section 2, 1.
70. Cole, *Century Has Passed*, 25.

71. "50,000 Loss Is Result of Big Fire at Duncan," *Copper Era*, February 4, 1921, 1.

72. Foote, *Century and More*, 9.

73. "J.A. Billingsley & Co," *Copper Era*, December 10, 1908, 3.

74. "Local and Personal," *Duncan Arizonian*, January 17, 1912, 1.

75. Cole, *Century Has Passed*, 22.

76. "Sells Drug Store," *Copper Era*, September 29, 1916, 1.

77. Cole, *Century Has Passed*, 96–97.

78. "Hal Empie (1909–2002)."

79. "50,000 Loss Is Result of Big Fire at Duncan."

80. "The Duncan Hotel," *Copper Era*, May 14, 1908, 4.

81. "Mines and Mining," *Copper Era*, January 2, 1902, 3.

82. "Notice—Duncan Dinner," *Copper Era*, November 21, 1907, 2.

83. "Splendid Hobbs Hotel Is Soon Open to Public," *Copper Era*, January 30, 1914, 3.

84. "Supervisor Witt Buys Hobbs Hotel," *Copper Era*, March 26, 1915, 3.

85. "Buys Valley Hotel," *Copper Era*, September 1, 1916, 4.

86. "Simpson Hotel," *Copper Era*, August 4, 1922, 3.

87. "Purely Personal," *Copper Era*, August 27, 1908, 3.

88. "Duncan Dots," *Copper Era*, September 13, 1912, 6.

89. Cole, *Century Has Passed*, 41.

90. "The Duncan Saloon," *Copper Era*, December 19, 1913, 17.

91. "Auditor's Report on Accounts of Greenlee County, Arizona for the Month of June 1914," *Copper Era*, July 31, 1914, 10.

92. Cole, *Century Has Passed*, 106.

93. "Notice for Bids," *Graham Guardian*, June 19, 1908, 4.

94. "Duncan," *Arizona Republic*, September 30, 1953, 8.

95. "Duncan High School," *Copper Era*, May 28, 1915, 5.

96. "High School Contract Let," *Copper Era*, July 9, 1915, 5.

97. "Dedication of Union High School," *Copper Era*, April 7, 1916, 2

98. "High School at Duncan Reduced to Ashes," *Copper Era*, November 21, 1919, 1.

99. Cole, *Century Has Passed*, 106.

100. "Contract Awarded," *Copper Era*, January 7, 1921, 5.

101. "Third Annual County Fair Tomorrow," *Copper Era*, November 4, 1921, 1.

102. "Gets Virden School," *Carlsbad (NM) Current-Argus*, September 2, 1955, 12.

103. "New Duncan School," *Arizona Republican*, October 4, 1926, section 1, 4.

104. "February," *Duncan Wildcat* (Duncan High School), 1939, 30.

105. "Duncan Grabs Third Straight State Title," *Arizona Daily Star*, March 3, 1940, 11.

106. "Gene O'Dell Signs with Pro Cagers," *Arizona Daily Sun* (Flagstaff, AZ), July 19, 1948, 5.

107. "Virden Defeats Albuquerque Indians for State Cage Title," *Albuquerque (NM) Journal*, March 11, 1934, 4.

108. "Little Virden Marches Home with State Title," *Albuquerque (NM) Tribune*, March 13, 1944, 8.

109. "Duncan Completing $170,000 Gymnasium," *Arizona Daily Sun*, August 3, 1949, 8.

110. "Texas Western Edges Sun Devil Quint, 67–61," *Arizona Republic*, December 2, 1949, 19.

111. Lunt.

112. "Round about Town," *Copper Era*, August 9, 1912, 5.

113. "News from Duncan," *Copper Era*, August 16, 1912, 6.

114. Cole, *Century Has Passed*, 138.

115. "Local and Personal," *Duncan Arizonian*, August 21, 1912, 1.

116. "School Expenditures for the Month of January," *Copper Era*, April 10, 1914, 9.

117. "To Bridge the Gila," *Copper Era*, October 15, 1903, 4.

118. "Duncan Bridge Finished," *Duncan Arizonian*, July 24, 1912, 1.

119. "Duncan to Celebrate," *Copper Era*, September 10, 1915, 1.

120. "Frisco River again Breaks Over Its Banks," *Copper Era*, October 13, 1916, 1.

121. "Gila River Bridge Nears Completion," *Arizona Republic*, May 11, 1950, 2.

122. Fraser, "Arizona Historic Bridge Inventory Greenlee County," 414.

123. "An Awful Mine Disaster," *Copper Era*, February 21, 1901, 2.

124. "Mines and Mining," *Copper Era*, July 26, 1906, 3.

125. "New Ash Peak School," *Copper Era*, November 23, 1917, 5.

126. Cole, *Century Has Passed*, 99.

127. "H. Lesinsky," *Arizona Daily Star*, July 9, 1879, 2.

128. *Duncan Valley News*, 1.

129. Barnes, *Arizona Place Names*, 171.

130. Burgess, *Mt. Graham Profiles*, 261.

131. Cole, *Century Has Passed*, 96.

132. Barnes, *Arizona Place Names*, 167.

133. Myrick, *Railroads of Arizona*, 65.

134. "Telephone to Guthrie," *Copper Era*, June 15, 1917, 5.

135. "Local News," *Osage (KS) City Free Press*, August 15, 1889, 5.

Chapter 2

136. Burgess, *Mt. Graham Profiles*, 199–200.
137. "Clifton," *Borderer* (Las Cruces, NM), August 9, 1873, University of New Mexico, 1.
138. "Clifton Copper Mines," *Arizona Citizen*, November 21, 1874, 1.
139. "Arizona Copper Co.," *Tucson Citizen*, January 7, 1883, 3.
140. "Mining News," *Oasis* (Nogales, AZ), May 3, 1902, 10.
141. "Big New Smelter Will Blow in This Month," *Copper Era*, August 8, 1913, 1.
142. "Copper Mountain Mining District," *Arizona Citizen*, December 14, 1872, 2.
143. "Mining," *Arizona Daily Star*, June 5, 1883, 4.
144. "Graham County," *Arizona Weekly Citizen*, February 2, 1884, 2.
145. "Funeral Is Held for Woman, 102," *Arizona Republic*, August 14, 1941, section 2, 1.
146. "County Records," *Daily Tombstone* (Tombstone, AZ), September 10, 1886, 3.
147. "Lonely Landmark," *Arizona Days & Ways*, supplement to the *Arizona Republic*, July 29, 1962, 4.
148. "Metcalf School Building Razed," *Arizona Republic*, July 11, 1940, section 2, 1.
149. "Metcalf-Ghostless Ghost Mining Camp," *Arizona Republic*, February 9, 1950, 6.
150. Barnes, *Arizona Place Names*, 165.
151. "Local Items," *Copper Era*, November 18, 1910, 3.
152. "Rock Goes Through Post Office Roof," *Arizona Republican*, September 9, 1925, 4.
153. "Pioneer Editor Dies in Tucson," *Arizona Daily Star*, February 15, 1948, section A, 1.
154. "Post Office Rites Friday," *Tucson (AZ) Daily Citizen*, June 26, 1957, 31.
155. Barnes, *Arizona Place Names*, 169.
156. "Phelps Dodge Reports Gains in Past Year," *Tucson Daily Citizen*, March 28, 1949, 24.

157. "Morenci to Dedicate Post Office Situated on New Townsite," *Arizona Republic*, August 3, 1968, 10.

158. Barnes, *Arizona Place Names*, 169.

159. "Post Office at Metcalf Closed After 37 Years," *Copper Era*, May 23, 1936, Arizona Historical Society Library & Archives, 1.

160. "Lovely Lady and a Ghostless Ghost Town," Arizona Days and Ways, supplement to the *Arizona Republic*, June 12, 1955, 2.

161. "The Summer Widowers," *Copper Era*, July 27, 1905, 2.

162. "To Summer Widowers," *Copper Era*, July 5, 1906, 4.

163. "Our Mineral Belt and Its History," *Copper Era*, May 15, 1902, 1.

164. "Basketball Tonight," *Bisbee (AZ) Daily Review*, February 17, 1905, 5.

165. Clark, interview with Filmore and Yiada Stanton.

166. "A New Theatre Will Open Saturday Night," *Copper Era*, August 27, 1908, 3.

167. "Children's Prize Night," *Copper Era*, September 10, 1908, 3.

168. "Flying Machines," *Copper Era*, June 17, 1909, 5.

169. "High School Commencement," *Copper Era*, June 2, 1911, 1.

170. "Five Buildings Burn in Clifton; Damage Estimated at $9,000," *Arizona Republic*, December 2, 1924, section 1, 7.

171. "Spirited Runaway of Delivery Horse," *Copper Era*, September 6, 1912, 1.

172. "Elephant Intelligence," *Copper Era*, August 30, 1912, 5.

173. "New Princess Theatre," *Copper Era*, July 18, 1913, 7.

174. "Stage Set for Celebration on July 4," *Copper Era*, June 29, 1935, Arizona Historical Society Library & Archives, 1.

175. "Tennis Games at Night Is Novel Morenci Sport," *Arizona Daily Star*, October 4, 1914, section A, 9.

176. "Grand Labor Day Celebration Monday," *Copper Era*, September 1, 1916, 1.

177. "Gen. Manager Carmichael Entertains Returning Soldier Boys," *Copper Era*, June 27, 1919, 5.

178. "Relay Race," *Copper Era*, March 5, 1920, 1.

179. "Clifton Wins Relay Race," *Copper Era*, November 26, 1920, 1.

180. "Concrete Bridge Open to Public," *Copper Era*, September 13, 1918, 1.

181. "Ground to Be Broken at Clifton Today for Hot Springs Bathhouse," *Arizona Republican*, June 18, 1928, section 1, 6.

182. "Copies of *Arizona Republican* Go into Clifton Cornerstone," *Arizona Republican*, August 8, 1928, section 1, 5.

183. "Giant Copper Plate for Bathhouse Cornerstone at Clifton Is Finished," *Arizona Republican*, August 10, 1928, section 2, 1.

184. "Remodel City Park at Clifton to Provide Gateway for Town," *Arizona Republican*, May 1, 1930, section 1, 6.

185. Lunt.

186. "Clifton Theater Vandalized; Morenci 'Gang War' Flares," *Arizona Republic*, January 10, 1958, 1.

187. "Duncan Five Gives Globe Trotters First Defeat in 89," *Copper Era*, February 20, 1948, Arizona Historical Society Library & Archives, 9.

188. "Morenci," *Arizona Republic*, September 30, 1953, 8.

189. Lunt.

190. Colquhoun, *History of the Clifton-Morenci Mining District*, 21.

191. Lunt.

192. "Minor Mention," *Copper Era*, September 30, 1909, 3.

193. "Exceeded Speed Limit," *Copper Era*, July 8, 1910, 3.

194. "Clifton Hotel, Old Landmark, Destroyed by Spectacular Fire," *Copper Era*, April 2, 1932, Arizona Historical Society Library & Archives, 1.

195. Graham and Kupel, *Historical American Buildings Survey HABS No. AZ-188*.

196. "Morenci Hotel," *Arizona Bulletin Supplement Souvenir Edition*, 19.

197. "Items of Local Interest," *Copper Era*, February 27, 1920, 6.

198. "W.A. Pitt Hurt by Fall," *Copper Era*, July 25, 1907, 3.

199. "Hotel Reardon to Soon Open," *Copper Era*, August 22, 1913, 4.

200. "Incipient Fire at Reardon," *Copper Era*, January 30, 1914, 5.

201. "Feeding Prisoners," *Copper Era*, January 21, 1916, 2.

202. "Southern Pacific Conductor Killed in Fall from Car," *Arizona Republican*, August 21, 1927, section 1, 3.

203. "Court Matters," *Tombstone Epitaph* (Tombstone, AZ), June 25, 1899, 1.

204. Lunt.

205. "Minor Mention," *Copper Era*, November 20, 1902, 3.

206. Graham and Kupel, *Historical American Buildings Survey HABS No. AZ-193*.

207. "Arizona News," *Oasis*, May 13, 1899, 12.

208. *Copper Era*, March 1, 1900, 4.

209. Lunt.

210. *History of the Sacred Heart Parish Clifton*, Arizona, 9.

211. "New Catholic Church Is Dedicated," *Copper Era*, March 16, 1917, 4.

212. "Beautiful Church for Catholics of Morenci," *Copper Era*, October 10, 1913, 5.

213. *Souvenir of the Observance of the Golden Jubilee Holy Cross Parish, Morenci, Arizona*, 26.

214. "Morenci: Where They're Moving a Town to Make Room for a New Mine," *Arizona Daily Star*, May 25, 1972, section 4, 5.

215. "The Story True," *Graham Guardian*, December 27, 1895, 1.

216. "Details of Chacon's Capture," *Bisbee Daily Review*, September 7, 1902, 4.

217. "Chacon Hanged," *Copper Era*, November 27, 1902, 2.

218. *Amazing Arizona!*, 79–80.

219. Adams, "Prison in the Solid Rock," 265–68.

220. "Jail Blasted Out of Solid Rock at Clifton Preserved as Tourist Attraction," *Arizona Republican*, June 26, 1929, section 2, 5.

221. Colquhoun, *History of the Clifton-Morenci Mining District*, 23–31.

222. "Duel to the Death Fought at Morenci," *Copper Era*, April 7, 1911, 1.

223. "Sheriff McBride and Two Deputies Killed in Battle with Powers Boys in Their Home in Graham Mountains," *Copper Era*, February 15, 1918, 1.

224. Letter from Brigadier General Wolcott B. Hayes to William R. Ridgway.

225. "Powers-Sisson Outlaws Are Captured by Border Patrol near Hachita, N.M.," *Copper Era*, March 8, 1918, 1.

226. "Powers-Sisson Bandits Are Brought to Clifton Jail," *Copper Era*, March 15, 1918, 1.

227. "Clifton Town Hall Is the Finest in the State," *Copper Era*, April 2, 1920, 1.

228. Redford.

229. "Morenci Schools Opening Dates," *Copper Era*, July 30, 1969, Arizona Historical Society Library & Archives, 1.

230. "Morenci School Notes," *Copper Era*, February 22, 1918, 6.

231. "Summary of Work in Schools for Past Year," *Copper Era*, May 19, 1916, 4.

232. "Morenci News," *Copper Era*, November 21, 1901, 2.

233. "New School for Morenci," *El Paso (TX) Herald*, September 25, 1907, 10.

234. *Clifton Schools Centennial 1882–1982*, 5.

235. "Contractor Merritt Departs," *Copper Era*, March 5, 1908, 3.

236. "South Clifton School," *Copper Era*, March 5, 1908, 3.

237. "Minor Mention," *Copper Era*, March 12, 1908, 3.

238. Myrick, *Railroads of Arizona*, 87.

239. *Clifton Schools Centennial 1882–1982*, 5.

240. "Clifton Obtains Band Building," *Arizona Republic*, November 1, 1941, section 1, 14.

241. "Repairs Made on Clifton High School," *Arizona Republic*, September 13, 1962, 37.

242. Lunt.

243. Fuller.

244. Clifton Recreational Park, stadium dedication plaque.

245. Lunt.

246. *Clifton Schools Centennial 1882–1982*, 8.

247. "Morenci Jr.-Sr. High School Nears Completion; Will Be Ready for Fall School Term," *Copper Era*, August 19, 1949, Arizona Historical Society Library & Archives, 1.

248. "3-Game Tour Set for Jacks This Weekend," *Arizona Daily Sun*, December 13, 1949, 7.

249. "This Is It!," *Copper Cat* (Morenci High School), 1982, 164.

250. "Phelps Dodge Reports Gains in Past Year," *Tucson (AZ) Daily Citizen*, March 28, 1949, 24.

251. "Strayed or Lost!," *Copper Era*, August 12, 1909, 3.

252. "Accident of Metcalf Incline," *Copper Era*, August 1, 1907, 3.

253. "William J. Bryan," *Copper Era*, November 25, 1909, 2, 4.

254. "Nine Men Killed Instantly When Ore Cars Dash Down Coronado Incline," *Copper Era*, August 15, 1913, 1.

255. Barnes, *Arizona Place Names*, 165.

256. Myrick, *Railroads of Arizona*, 312.

257. "Smelter Rumor Is Finally Put at Rest," *Copper Era*, January 17, 1913, 1.

258. "Old A.C. Smelter Passes into History," *Copper Era*, January 2, 1914, 1.

259. Clark, interview with Filmore and Yiada Stanton.

260. "Clifton Smelter Blown In," *Arizona Republican*, August 31, 1913, 14.

261. Cogut and Conger, *History of Arizona's Clifton-Morenci Mining District*, 67.

262. "Detroit Copper Company's Concentrator," *Arizona Silver Belt* (Globe, AZ), June 8, 1899, 4.

263. Myrick, *Railroads of Arizona*, 80, 83.

264. "Phelps Dodge in Expansion Step," *Los Angeles Times*, May 4, 1931, 13.

265. "Work Starts on Tunnel to Drain Clifton-Morenci Mine," *Arizona Daily Star*, January 22, 1928, section 3, 1.

266. "Morenci's Copper Bolsters America," *Arizona Republic*, February 22, 1942, section 5, 4.

267. "P-D Plans Expansion at Morenci," *Arizona Daily Star*, August 17, 1968, section 2, 1.

268. "PD to Shut Down Morenci Smelter," *Arizona Daily Star*, December 22, 1984, section 1, 1.

269. "Morenci Smelter Is Now Just a Memory," *Morenci (AZ) Copper Review*, November 1996, 1.

270. "General Office for D.C.M. Co. at Morenci," *Copper Era*, August 15, 1913, 3.

271. "Minor Mention," *Copper Era*, February 25, 1904, 3.

272. "Minor Mention," *Copper Era*, June 9, 1904, 3.

273. "Minor Mention," *Copper Era*, February 10, 1910, 3.

274. Hunt.

275. "Walter C. Lawson."

276. "Charles E. Mills."

277. Cogut and Conger, *History of Arizona's Clifton-Morenci Mining District*, 170.

278. "Merchants Prepare to Move in August," *Copper Era*, July 26, 1967, Arizona Historical Society Library & Archives, 1.

279. "Minor Mention," *Copper Era*, June 9, 1904, 3.

280. "Mines and Mining," *Copper Era*, March 1, 1900, 7.

281. Burgess, *Mt. Graham Profiles*, 106–7.

282. *Clifton Clarion*, January 20, 1886, 3.

283. "Opening Guns Are Fired by State Candidates," *Copper Era*, October 8, 1920, 1.

284. "Adios Clifton," *Arizona Republican*, March 23, 1898, 3.

285. "Colquhoun Dinner," *Copper Era*, January 17, 1901, 3.

286. "Morenci Items," *Copper Era*, March 1, 1900, 5.

287. "Detroit Copper Mining Company's Store," *Arizona Bulletin Supplement Souvenir Edition*, 17.

288. *Portrait and Biological Record of Arizona*, 636.

289. "Minor Mention," *Copper Era*, September 12, 1901, 3.

290. Graham and Kupel, *Historical American Buildings Survey HABS No. AZ-197*.

291. "Charles Spezia's Walking Tour of Historic Chase Creek, Clifton Arizona, 1900–29," items 5 and 7.

292. "New Bank Opens for Business," *Copper Era*, March 8, 1918, 1.

293. Nabor and Nabor.

294. Norton.

295. "Morenci Gets New Building," *Arizona Republic*, August 31, 1947, section 3, 12.

296. Graham and Kupel, *Historical American Buildings Survey HABS No. AZ-199*.

297. Graham and Kupel, *Historical American Buildings Survey HABS No. AZ-174-E*.

298. "War Garden Is Making Good," *Copper Era*, August 17, 1917, 1.

299. "Residence for Gen. Manager Carmichael," *Copper Era*, July 18, 1913, 7.

300. Graham and Kupel, *Historical American Buildings Survey HABS No. AZ-174-F*.

301. "Bullets Fired at Residence of Carmichael," *Copper Era*, March 31, 1916, 1.

302. "Shannon Heights to Become a City," *Copper Era*, December 20, 1906, 3.
303. "Contract Let for 50 Homes," *Tucson Daily Citizen*, August 3, 1937, 3.
304. "Witches in State? Could Be," *Arizona Republic*, December 7, 1963, 21.
305. "Organize Club," *Arizona Daily Star*, May 8, 1939, 9.
306. "Once-Barren Land Grows Many Flowers for Stargo Exhibition," *Arizona Republic*, June 2, 1941, 5.
307. "P.W. Womack Gets Contract," *Arizona Republic*, March 24, 1940, section 2, 6.
308. Burgess, *Mt. Graham Profiles*, 48–49.
309. "Arizona News Views and Gossip," *Tucson Citizen*, December 17, 1901, 5.
310. Myrick, *Railroads of Arizona*, 158.
311. "Good Road Practically Complete from Clifton to Graham Connecting Greenlee with Central Arizona," *Bisbee Daily Review*, September 12, 1920, section 2, 3.
312. "Dell M. Potter Speaks to Enthusiastic Crowd in Metcalf," *Copper Era*, October 25, 1912, 5.
313. Du Shane, "Charles Allen Hamblin Gravesite."
314. "Longest State Tunnel Ready," *Arizona Republic*, July 24, 1949, section 1, 1.
315. Cole, *Century Has Passed*, 258.
316. "'Black Jack's' Death," *Arizona Daily Star*, May 9, 1897, 1.
317. "The Lesinsky Railway," *Arizona Citizen*, June 20, 1879, 1.
318. Myrick, *Railroads of Arizona*, 201.
319. "Fatal Accident," *Copper Era*, May 17, 1900, 2.
320. "Morenci Is Busy in Construction," *Copper Era*, July 18, 1913, 2.
321. Myrick, *Railroads of Arizona*, 313.
322. "Clifton Visited by Another Great Flood," *Copper Era*, December 6, 1906, 1.
323. "The Chase Creek Wall," *Copper Era*, February 17, 1910, 3.
324. "High Water Causes Grave Alarm to Residents," *Copper Era*, January 21, 1916, 1.
325. "Morenci Now Surrounded by Soldiers," *Bisbee Daily Review*, June 12, 1903, 1.
326. Burgess, *Mt. Graham Profiles*, 480.
327. "Unprecedented Disaster," *Copper Era*, June 11, 1903, 2.
328. "A.&N.M. Engine Crew Assaulted by Strikers," *Copper Era*, October 8, 1915, 1.
329. "Duncan Tent Colony Offers Cozy Refuge for All Who Quit Oppression of Clifton Strike," *Bisbee Daily Review*, October 31, 1915, section 2, 1.

330. "Guard to Go Inside P-D Gates," *Arizona Daily Star*, August 19, 1983, section 1, 1.

331. "Clifton Sheet 1."

332. "Minor Mention," *Copper Era*, August 13, 1903, 3.

333. "Accident on Longfellow Incline," *Copper Era*, August 1, 1907, 3.

334. "Territorial News," *Bisbee Daily Review*, July 11, 1902, 5.

335. "Grand Jury Adds Seven New Cases to Docket," *Copper Era*, May 16, 1919, 1.

336. "New Hospital at Morenci Now in Commission," *Copper Era*, February 7, 1940, Arizona Historical Society Library & Archives, 1.

337. "Home-Coming Luncheon Is First Social Event of Morenci Club," *Arizona Republic*, October 12, 1940, section 1, 11.

338. "Morenci's Old Hospital En Route to Ft. Grant," *Arizona Daily Star*, December 18, 1969, section 2, 1.

339. "New $1,800,000 Hospital Opens in Morenci," *Copper Era*, February 21, 1968, Arizona Historical Society Library & Archives, 1.

340. "Morenci News," *Copper Era*, June 18, 1903, 2.

341. *Arizona Army National Guard*, 45–46.

342. "General Tuthill to Practice Medicine in Phoenix," *Copper Era*, June 13, 1919, 2.

343. "Tuthill Is Named as Health Chief," *Copper Era*, July 22, 1921, 3.

344. *Arizona Army National Guard*, 48.

345. "Last of Class 1 Go to Camp Cody," *Copper Era*, May 31, 1918, 1.

346. "In Memoriam of W.W. Colquhoun," *Copper Era*, July 11, 1919, 1.

Chapter 3

347. "First State Fish Hatchery to Be Ready on Sept. 1," *Morning Sun* (Yuma, AZ), August 23, 1923, 4.

348. "Greenlee County," *Arizona Republic*, May 19, 1946, section 2, 3.

349. "Maddock Inspects Springerville Highway," *Copper Era*, May 12, 1922, 1.

350. "Clifton Contractors Win with Bid on Road," *Arizona Republican*, May 23, 1926, section 1, 8.

351. Waite, "History of Hannagan Meadow Lodge," 1–2.

352. "Indian Dance to Start Highway Festival Today," *Arizona Daily Star*, June 19, 1926, 3.

353. Waite, "History of Hannagan Meadow Lodge," 8.

354. "Proceedings of the Board of Supervisors," *Copper Era*, July 15, 1909, 2.

355. "County Expenditures for 1915 Estimated by Board at $347,955.77," *Copper Era*, July 10, 1914, 1.

356. Fitch and Ewing, *Heart and Hub of Eagle Creek*, 231–51.

357. *Duncan to Alpine*, tape 2, side A, 25:25.

358. "The Home Copper Company," *Copper Era*, January 9, 1902, 2.

359. "Eagle Creek to Have New Ranger Station," *Arizona Republican*, October 6, 1926, section 1, 4.

360. "Honeymoon Lives On: Character of Secluded Arizona Town Remains Rugged, Individualistic," *Tucson Citizen*, November 15, 1991, section D, 14.

361. "Toga May Wheatley," *Arizona Republic*, September 25, 1961, 27.

362. Waite, "History of Hannagan Meadow Lodge," 2–3.

363. "Arizona Pioneer Tells of Raid by Murderous Apache Band," *Arizona Republic*, April 14, 1937, section 2, 7.

364. "C.C.C. Progress for Area Told," *Arizona Daily Star*, June 1, 1933, 3.

365. "CCC Camps Arizona."

366. "The Big Parade Explores Arizona," *Arizona Republic*, June 24, 1934, section 4, 6.

367. "Photos Arizona."

368. "Football Suits Are Donated by Morenci," *Copper Era*, October 12, 1935, Arizona Historical Society Library & Archives, AZ, 1.

369. "CCC Group Is Graduated," *Arizona Republic*, October 8, 1940, section 2, 7.

BIBLIOGRAPHY

Adams, Theodore. "A Prison in the Solid Rock." *Wide World Magazine* (1904), 265–68.

Amazing Arizona! Historical Markers in Arizona. Vol. 1. Arizona Development Board (1957), 79–80.

Arizona Army National Guard: The First One Hundred Years, Pamphlet Number 870-5. 180th Field Artillery Regiment Association, February 22, 2002.

Arizona Bulletin Supplement Souvenir Edition (Solomonville, AZ), 1903. University of Arizona Libraries.

Arizona Historical Society Library & Archives. Tucson, Arizona.

Barnes, Will C. *Arizona Place Names.* Tucson: University of Arizona Press, 1960.

Burgess, Glen, ed. *Mt. Graham Profiles.* Vol. 2, *Ryder Ridgway Collection.* Graham County Historical Society, January 1, 1988.

"Charles E. Mills." Mining Foundation of the Southwest. Accessed September 16, 2019. https://www.miningfoundationsw.org/Charles_Mills.

"Charles Spezia's Walking Tour of Historic Chase Creek, Clifton Arizona, 1900–29." Greenlee County Historical Society, Clifton, Arizona, 1990.

Civilian Conservation Corps Legacy. "CCC Camps Arizona." Accessed September 15, 2017. https://ccclegacy.org/ccc-camp-lists/camp-list-arizona/.

———. "Photos Arizona." Accessed September 15, 2017. https://ccclegacy.org/history-center/photos-by-state/photos-arizona/.

Clark, Jayne. Interview with Filmore and Yiada Stanton, 1975.

Clifton Recreational Park. Stadium dedication plaque, 1936.

Clifton Schools Centennial 1882–1982, Collector's Edition to The Copper Era (Clifton, AZ), November 10, 1982.

"Clifton Sheet 1." Sanborn-Perris Map Company, April 1893.

Cogut, Ted, and Bill Conger. *History of Arizona's Clifton-Morenci Mining District—A Personal Approach.* Volume 2, *The Era of Mining by Open Pit.* Thatcher, AZ: Mining History, 1999.

Cole, Helen, ed. *A Century Has Passed: Duncan Centennial 1883–1983.* Duncan, AZ: Duncan Centennial Committee, 1984.

Colquhoun, James. *The History of the Clifton-Morenci Mining District.* London, UK: William Clowes and Sons, 1924.

Copper Cat (Morenci High School yearbook), 1982.

Duncan to Alpine: The Coronado Trail. Phoenix, AZ: Sound Travel Ideas, 1994.

Duncan Valley News. Special edition of the *Copper Era* (Clifton, AZ), August 3, 1983.

The Duncan Wildcat (Duncan High School yearbook), 1939.

Du Shane, Neal. "Charles Allen Hamblin Gravesite." American Pioneer & Cemetery Research Project. Accessed August 25, 2017. www.apcrp.org.

Fitch, Edie, and Pamela Ewing, illus. *The Heart and Hub of Eagle Creek.* Tucson, AZ: Wild West Print Communications, 2006.

Foote, Wally, ed. *A Century and More.* Duncan, AZ: Duncan Historical Book Committee, 1993.

Fraser, Clayton B. "Arizona Historic Bridge Inventory Greenlee County." State of Arizona Historic Property Inventory Form. Loveland, CO: FRASERdesign, 1994.

Fuller, Mike. Conversation with authors, December 9, 2021.

Graham, Robert G., and Douglas Kupel. Historical American Buildings Survey HABS No. AZ-174-E. Phoenix, AZ: Ryden Architects, 1994.

———. Historical American Buildings Survey HABS No. AZ-174-F. Phoenix, AZ: Ryden Architects, 1994.

———. Historical American Buildings Survey HABS No. AZ-188. Phoenix, AZ: Ryden Architects, 1994.

———. Historical American Buildings Survey HABS No. AZ-193. Phoenix, AZ: Ryden Architects, 1994.

———. Historical American Buildings Survey HABS No. AZ-197. Phoenix, AZ: Ryden Architects, 1994.

———. Historical American Buildings Survey HABS No. AZ-199. Phoenix, AZ: Ryden Architects, 1994.

Greenlee County Historical Society. Clifton, Arizona.

Hal Empie Gallery. "Hal Empie (1909–2002)." Accessed August 28, 2021. www.halempiestudio-gallery.com.

"History of the Sacred Heart Parish." Sacred Heart Parish. Clifton, Arizona, October 1, 1950.

Hunt, Gerald D. Conversation with Robert A. Chilicky, November 30, 2017.

Letter from Brigadier General Wolcott B. Hayes to William R. Ridgway, March 9, 1949. In *The Power Family of Graham County Arizona*, by William "Ryder" Ridgway, with Milton Bean, 206–8. West Virginia: Texicanwife Books, 2012.

Lunt, Don. Conversation with authors, March 7, 2017.

Morenci Copper Review (Morenci, AZ), November 1996.

Myrick, David F. *Railroads of Arizona*. Vol. 3, *Clifton, Morenci and Metcalf Rails and Copper Mines*. Glendale, CA: Trans-Anglo Books, 1984.

Nabor, Ed, and Max Nabor. Conversation with authors, July 26, 2018.

Newspapers.com.

Norton, Jackie. Conversation with authors, September 15, 2020.

Patton, James Monroe. "The History of Clifton." Master's thesis, University of Arizona, 1945.

Portrait and Biological Record of Arizona. Chicago: Chapman Publishing Company, 1901.

Redford, Keith. Conversation with authors, February 19, 2019.

"Souvenir of the Observance of the Golden Jubilee Holy Cross Parish, Morenci, Arizona, December 17, 1963." Holy Cross Parish. Morenci, Arizona.

Waite, Tessa. "History of Lodge." Hannagan Meadow, 2003. Accessed September 15, 2018. https://hanaganmeadow.com/about/history-of-the-lodge/.

"Walter C. Lawson." National Mining Hall of Fame and Museum. Accessed September 16, 2019. https://www.mininghalloffame.org/hall-of-fame/walter-c-lawson.

ABOUT THE AUTHORS

Robert A. Chilicky was born in Morenci, Arizona, in 1970. He attended school in both Clifton and Morenci, graduating from Morenci High School in 1988. He enlisted in the United States Army, serving at Fort Sill, Oklahoma; Camp Stanley, South Korea; and Fort Polk, Louisiana. After four years, he enlisted into the Arizona National Guard for one year, then into the U.S. Army Reserve, where he has served for the last thirty years, with the current rank of master sergeant. He currently is employed by the Department of the Army, serving as a U.S. Army Reserve administrator. His education includes a bachelor of arts degree in history from the University of Arizona. He is currently completing requirements for a graduate certificate in archive studies and a master's degree in library and information science, also from the University of Arizona. He has coached high school softball and track and field and is a youth and high school football and softball official. He currently lives in Massachusetts and has four children and three grandchildren. Robert enjoyed growing up in the Clifton/Morenci area and has many fond memories of school and church activities and exploring the countryside. As a young person, he was aware of the history of the area and enjoyed hearing the stories from his father about the early mining companies. With this book he hopes that others will be inspired to further explore and research the rich history of the county.

G erald D. Hunt was born in 1946 in Lordsburg, New Mexico, where his family was involved in cattle ranching and owned several service stations. In 1950, his parents loaded the wagon and moved with Gerald and his sister, Sandy, to Morenci, Arizona. From an early age, one of his favorite pastimes was exploring old mine ruins and tunnels in the Clifton/Morenci/Metcalf area. He graduated from Morenci High School in 1964. Following graduation, Gerald served in the United States Navy, worked at the Morenci mine and attended Northern Arizona University, where he received two degrees and an educational administration certification. He also attended Western New Mexico University to earn New Mexico educational administration credentials. He taught at Nogales and Parker, Arizona; coached football, softball and cross country; was an instructor at Arizona Western College; and taught educational administration honorariums at the University of New Mexico. He lobbied for five years in Santa Fe and Washington, D.C., for public education. Before relocating to Washington State in 2001, Gerald was a principal, athletic director and director of the Federal Drug, Alcohol and Tobacco Prevention program at the New Mexico State Department of Education. Later, he served as an educational consultant in Washington. He received several honors and awards during his career in education, including selection as the New Mexico State Representative for Elementary Education Administration and recognition by the New Mexico legislature as Outstanding Administrator. Gerald is married to Diane Bryan and has six sons, nine grandchildren and two great-grandchildren. His hope is that people will enjoy reading about the county's history and will appreciate the archival photos in this book.